Easy-to-Make

Skateboards, Scooters and Racers

11 INEXPENSIVE PROJECTS

by

WILLIAM JABER

Dover Publications, Inc.
New York

To my grandson, Christopher James Semple

Born January 6, 1976 — a 20th Century child but a 21st Century man. May his future and that of all children be bright with promises fulfilled.

Published in Canada by General Publishing Company, Ltd., 30 Lesmill Road, Don Mills, Toronto, Ontario.
Published in the United Kingdom by Constable and Company, Ltd.

This Dover edition, first published in 1987, is an unabridged, slightly corrected republication of the work originally published by Drake Publishers, Inc., New York, in 1977 under the title *Wheels, Boxes, & Skateboards: How to Build Your Own Sidewalk Vehicles*. The present edition is published by special arrangement with Sterling Publishing Co., Inc., Two Park Avenue, New York, N.Y. 10016.

Manufactured in the United States of America
Dover Publications, Inc., 31 East 2nd Street, Mineola, N.Y. 11501

Library of Congress Cataloging-in-Publication Data

Jaber, William.
Easy-to-make skateboards, scooters and racers.

Reprint. Originally published: Wheels, boxes, & skateboards. New York : Drake Publishers, 1977.
1. Skateboards—Design and construction—Juvenile literature. 2. Scooters—Design and construction—Juvenile literature. 3. Automobiles—Models—Design and construction—Juvenile literature. I. Title.
TT174.5.S35J33   1987   688.6   87-602
ISBN 0-486-25376-7 (pbk.)

CONTENTS

INTRODUCTION

Anybody can go out and buy a wagon or a scooter. But if you really want to impress everybody on the block, make your own sidewalk vehicles. This book tells you how it can be done—how you can take junk and cast-off materials, and make real neat sidewalk jobs on wheels.

But you might now ask, "Where in the heck are we going to get a couple of good sets of matching wheels?" Well, the answer is easy! Just keep your eyes open and stay on good terms with all the neighbors, because there are more wheels on your block than in Macy's or Gimbels—you can bet on it. Just place your order by telling your neighbors to please reserve for you any sets of wheels they might have lying around. You might even offer to do some work for a couple of bucks—or a couple of wheels, and maybe one of their spare milk boxes or fruit boxes. That's the best way, but if you're really desperate, you might try to make a deal with Mom or Dad to buy a set of carriage wheels or buggy wheels. But it always makes us feel better if we do it ourselves—that way we don't owe anybody for it.

There's a TV ad that goes, ". . . When you've got your health, you've got just about everything. . . ." That may be very true, but it is equally true that if we have a good set of wheels, and we want to build a sidewalk vehicle, we, too, have "everything," because the wheels are the most important items. When they are available, planning a sidewalk vehicle is easier. What you are going to build depends a lot upon what kind of wheels you can come up with.

For example, if you have two shopping-cart wheels, like those on the two-wheel carts many people use for marketing, you have wheels that are just right for the two-wheel footboard scooter. These scooters are a lot of fun, but they are rare today.

But, suppose you could somehow get your hands on a set of four spoked wheels, like those on small bicycles— WOW! What we could do with those babies! They are ideal for the racer—a trim, fast soapbox racer. That would knock their eyes out. So, you see, it's all in what kind of wheels you can come up with. You can use any kind of wheels. There is a vehicle in this book for every kind of wheel—even for furniture casters.

One of the vehicles we are introducing in this book is a new kind of machine—one that will give a brand new meaning to sidewalks. We call it the "Whicky-Whack." If you can make one of these—and we show you how— you can be the hero to all the small children on the block, not to speak of all the boys—and girls—of your own age. The Whicky-Whack is to sidewalks what the Ferris wheel is to a carnival.

The main purpose of this book is not to introduce new things, however, but to show you what you can make with old things—with junk and cast-off materials. You need a large selection of boxes, boards, broomhandles, strips of plywood, scrap lumber and blocks of all sizes, plus paint, screws, nails, hooks, wire, string, bottlecaps—everything but the kitchen sink. That you won't need, except to wash your hands after handling all this junk.

The tools you will need include saws, hammers, pliers, screwdrivers, and other tools, most of which are valuable to your parents, and which had to be purchased by your parents. So they don't belong to you. Therefore, we advise you to avoid Dad and Mom having to yell at you because you were careless with the tools. Tools are not meant to play with—they are for useful work. Making a sidewalk vehicle is useful work only if the results are worth the effort and the trouble. You should take care of the tools and not cause too much trouble to your parents in the pursuit of the project. It is a fact that people who abuse machines and tools will also abuse other people, so don't put yourself in that group—you are made of better stuff.

The book is intended as a guide only. It points out some of the better ways to proceed in putting the vehicle together, and it suggests alternate methods from which you can choose. It also suggests materials, procedures, and provides the drawings that represent the author's best judgment, and are a product of the author's own experience as a boy. But you, the builder, should remain unimpressed with all this. You should pick and choose from what is offered, keeping in mind that the work at hand is your own, and not the work of the author. You must leave your own stamp on the work, and, in so doing, you will enjoy it much more.

TOOLS

These are the tools you will need most often. Do not use any electric tools or machines unless you have experience with them. Remember, on any job where you are not sure, get the advice of those who can help.

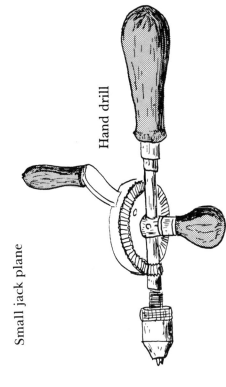

Small jack plane

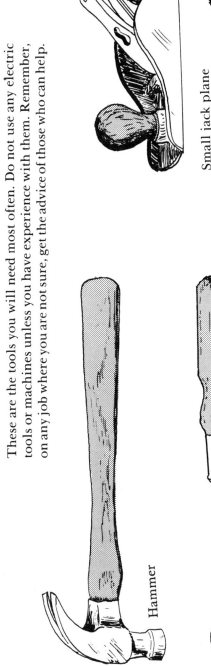

Hammer

Screwdriver

Pliers

Wood chisel

A 72-inch folding carpenter's rule

Hand drill

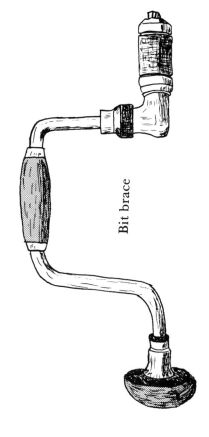

Bit brace

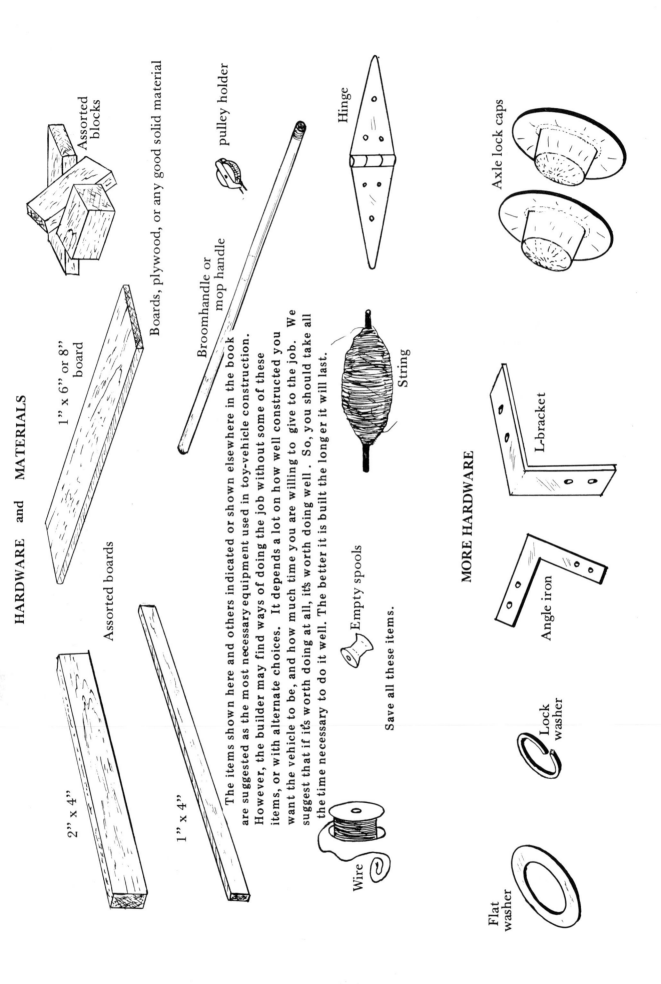

HARDWARE and MATERIALS

Assorted blocks

1" x 6" or 8" board

Boards, plywood, or any good solid material

pulley holder

Broomhandle or mop handle

Hinge

Axle lock caps

Assorted boards

2" x 4"

1" x 4"

The items shown here and others indicated or shown elsewhere in the book are suggested as the most necessary equipment used in toy-vehicle construction. However, the builder may find ways of doing the job without some of these items, or with alternate choices. It depends a lot on how well constructed you want the vehicle to be, and how much time you are willing to give to the job. We suggest that if it's worth doing at all, it's worth doing well. So, you should take all the time necessary to do it well. The better it is built the longer it will last.

String

Empty spools

Save all these items.

Wire

MORE HARDWARE

L-bracket

Angle iron

Flat washer

Lock washer

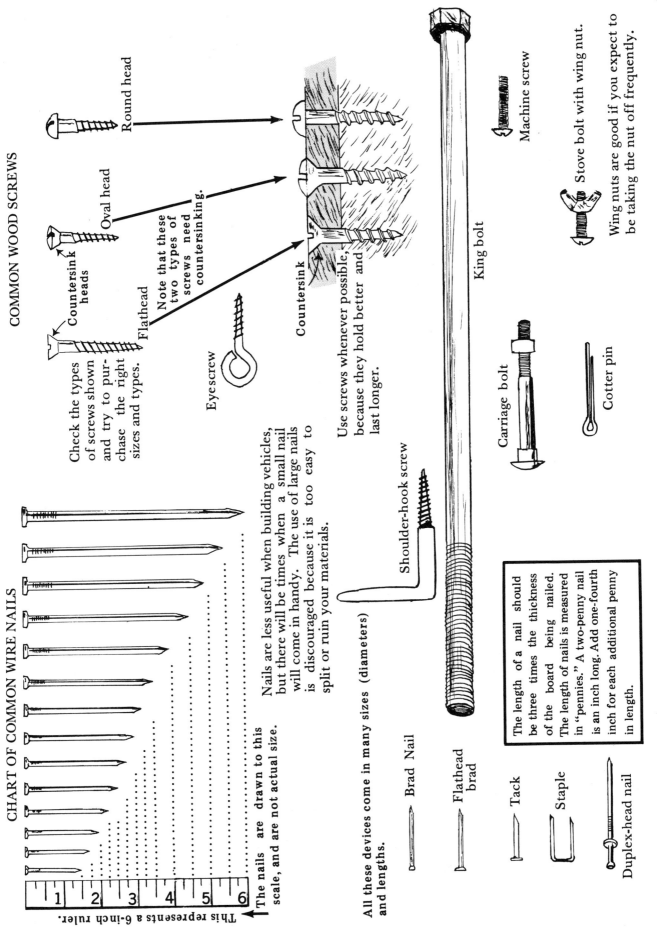

CHART OF COMMON WIRE NAILS

The nails are drawn to this scale, and are not actual size.

This represents a 6-inch ruler.

All these devices come in many sizes (diameters) and lengths.

Brad Nail

Flathead brad

Tack

Staple

Duplex-head nail

The length of a nail should be three times the thickness of the board being nailed. The length of nails is measured in "pennies." A two-penny nail is an inch long. Add one-fourth inch for each additional penny in length.

COMMON WOOD SCREWS

Round head

Oval head

Countersink heads

Flathead

Note that these two types of screws need countersinking.

Check the types of screws shown and try to purchase the right sizes and types.

Eyescrew

Countersink

Use screws whenever possible, because they hold better and last longer.

Nails are less useful when building vehicles, but there will be times when a small nail will come in handy. The use of large nails is discouraged because it is too easy to split or ruin your materials.

Shoulder-hook screw

King bolt

Carriage bolt

Cotter pin

Machine screw

Stove bolt with wing nut.

Wing nuts are good if you expect to be taking the nut off frequently.

3

SAWING   1
Some popular saws

Coping saw

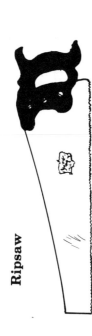

Designed for cutting curves and irregular shapes in the wood. Its teeth are similar to those of a crosscut saw.

Back saw or miter box saw

Used for making fine cuts. Its teeth are similar to those of a crosscut saw.

Keyhole saw

Similar to the coping saw in its use. Its teeth are like those of the ripsaw.

Ripsaw

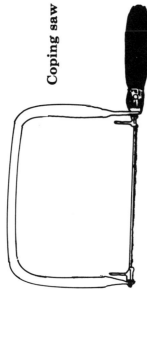

Used to cut along with the grain of the wood.

Crosscut saw

Used to cut across the grain of the wood.

Hacksaw

Used for cutting metal.

SAWING   2

Helpful hints for sawing

Use the proper kind of saw for a particular job. Most saws are classified as either ripsaws or crosscut saws. Like people, they can be identified by their teeth. The two main types of teeth used for common handsaws are shown here. The size of any saw is determined by the length of the blade in inches. Handsaws come in sizes 14 to 30 inches.

> Never cut metal with a saw that is designed to cut only wood.

CROSSCUT SAW

Each tooth is a two-edged knife which can cut in either direction. In the back stroke it scores ... makes a preliminary cut, so that in the main forward stroke the crosscut saw will cut deeply without splintering the wood. Because of this it is best for cutting across the grain of the wood.

The crosscut saw usually has 7 teeth per inch.

RIP SAW

Each tooth is a tiny chisel. Its cutting action is only in one direction. Each of the chisels cut out a piece of wood on the forward stroke. This is best for cutting with the grain.

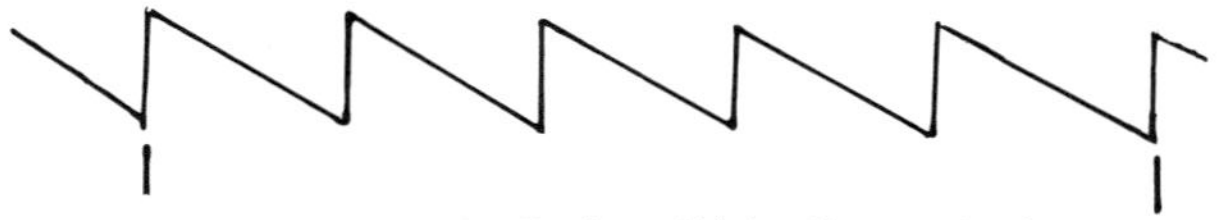

The ripsaw usually has 4½ teeth per inch.

WHEN A SAW BINDS OR STICKS

Do not force the blade. If the saw binds it indicates that one of three things is wrong: 1) the wood is too green; 2) the blade is rusted or is covered with some substance such as resin or oil; 3) the blade has too little "set"—the distance the teeth project to the sides. In the latter case, the blade has to be sharpened, and then reset.

HAMMERS and HAMMERING

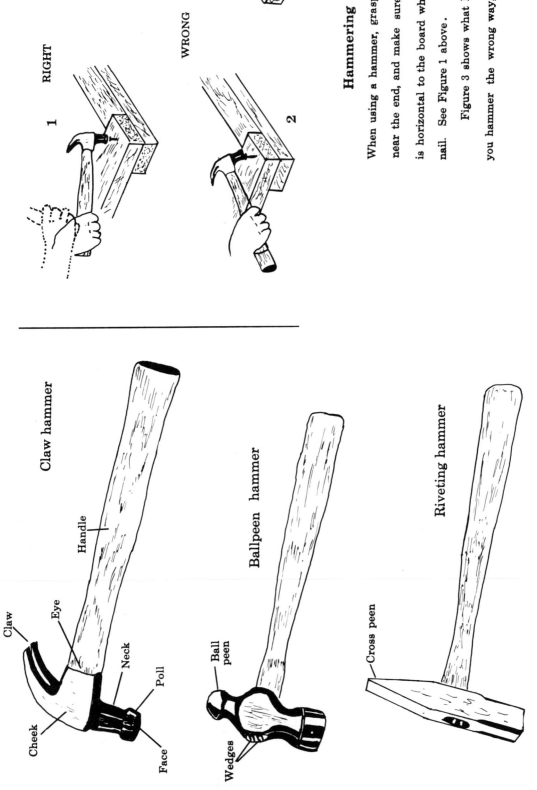

Claw hammer

Claw

Eye

Cheek

Neck

Poll

Face

Handle

Ballpeen hammer

Ball peen

Wedges

Riveting hammer

Cross peen

RIGHT

1

WRONG

2

3

Hammering

When using a hammer, grasp the handle near the end, and make sure the handle is horizontal to the board when it hits the nail. See Figure 1 above.

Figure 3 shows what happens when you hammer the wrong way, as in Fig. 2.

AXLES
THREE KINDS OF AXLES

Try to gather up an assortment of these.

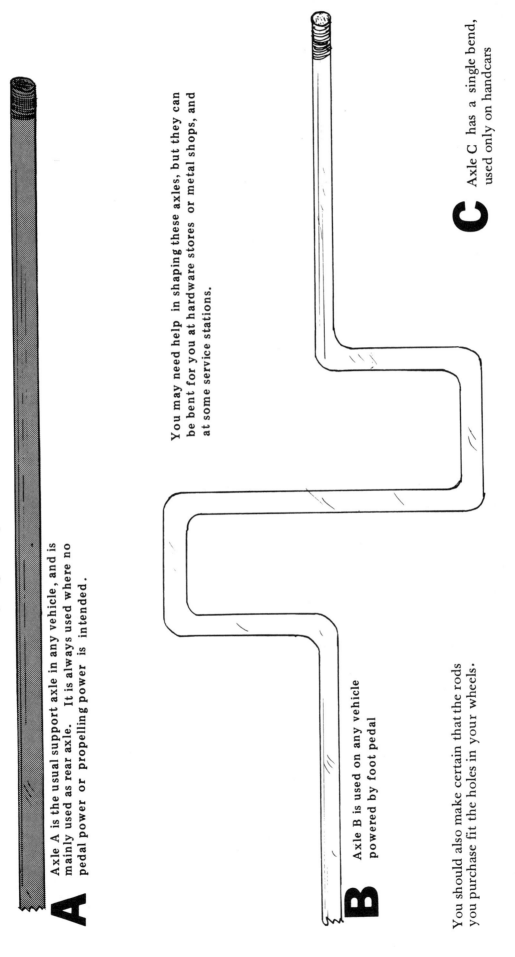

A   Axle A is the usual support axle in any vehicle, and is mainly used as rear axle. It is always used where no pedal power or propelling power is intended.

You may need help in shaping these axles, but they can be bent for you at hardware stores or metal shops, and at some service stations.

B   Axle B is used on any vehicle powered by foot pedal

You should also make certain that the rods you purchase fit the holes in your wheels.

C   Axle C has a single bend, used only on handcars

Axle rods will be hard to find. But if all else fails, rods of varying sizes, lengths and shapes can be purchased in hardware stores. Make sure the rods are of the right size to fit the nuts and washers you have.

THREE WAYS TO MOUNT AN AXLE ON AN AXLE TREE

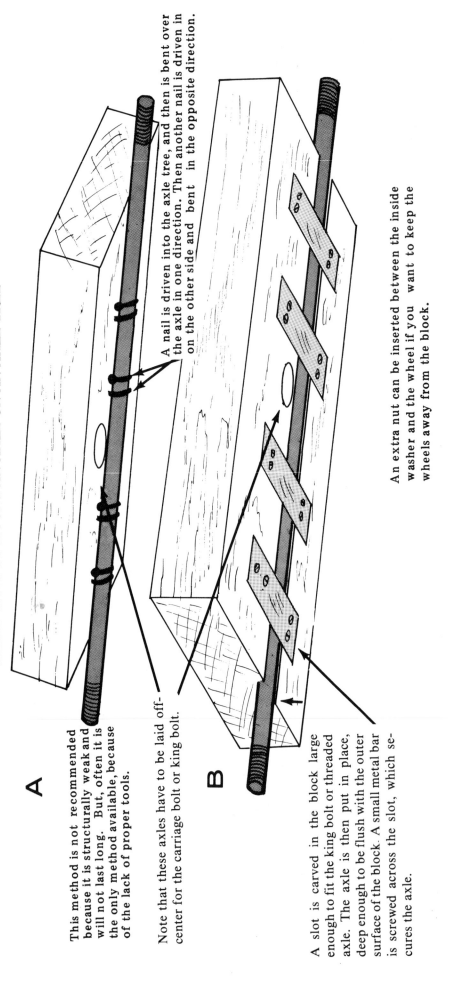

A

This method is not recommended because it is structurally weak and will not last long. But, often it is the only method available, because of the lack of proper tools.

Note that these axles have to be laid off-center for the carriage bolt or king bolt.

A nail is driven into the axle tree, and then is bent over the axle in one direction. Then another nail is driven in on the other side and bent in the opposite direction.

B

A slot is carved in the block large enough to fit the king bolt or threaded axle. The axle is then put in place, deep enough to be flush with the outer surface of the block. A small metal bar is screwed across the slot, which secures the axle.

An extra nut can be inserted between the inside washer and the wheel if you want to keep the wheels away from the block.

C

Short blocks for axle trees — one for each wheel. The blocks are mounted to the chassis.

Drill a hole in the axle tree to fit a king bolt, as shown. Be careful to make the hole just a bit smaller than the bolt, and insert the bolt as shown.

Threading — making grooves so that nuts can be put on — is done in most hardware shops for a small charge.

HOW TO ATTACH WHEELS TO THE AXLES

Wheel Mounting Method A

All the wheels in this book, except the skates, casters, and the footboard scooter wheels, are installed on the axle, using A or B methods. A is used if the axle has a hole for a cotter pin at the end, as shown.

Keep in mind that the best way to mount any wheel is to use a threaded axle, with nut and axle cap. Use the caps whether or not you use threaded axles, because the caps are a safety feature — they prevent injury to your shin and legs, or ripping your clothing.

A hole can be drilled in the end of the axle, but you may need help in doing this.   If getting the hole drilled is too much trouble, then use the axle cap only. But make certain that you have the proper size caps, and that they have been put on straight.

The cotter pin is used for a more secure wheel mounting.

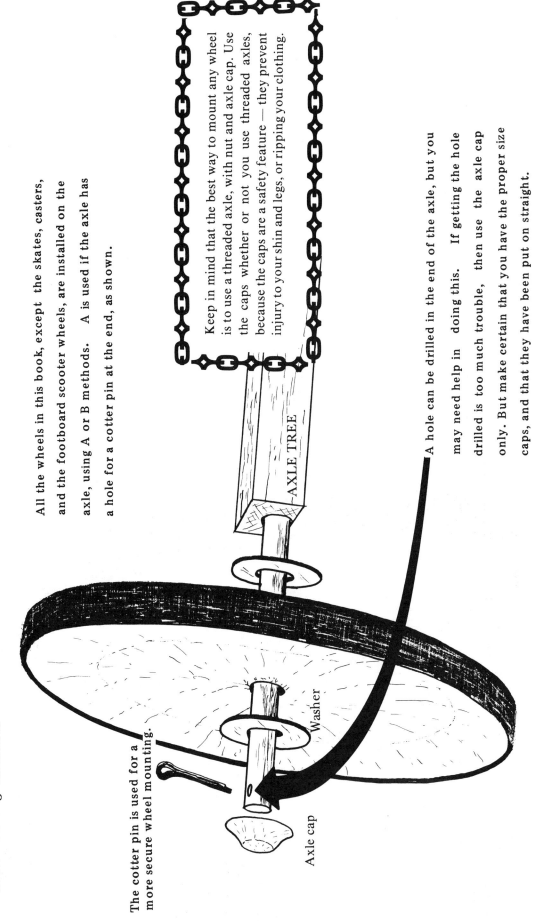

AXLE TREE

Washer

Axle cap

9

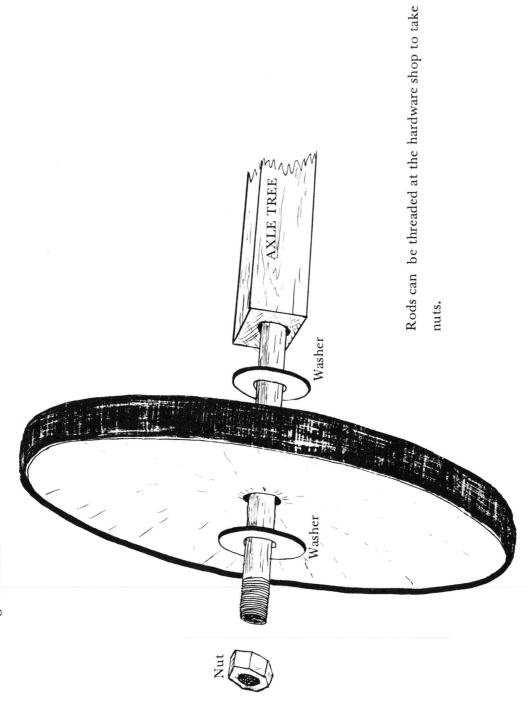

METHODS OF ATTACHING WHEELS

Wheel Mounting Method B

AXLE TREE

Washer

Washer

Nut

Rods can be threaded at the hardware shop to take nuts.

Wagon

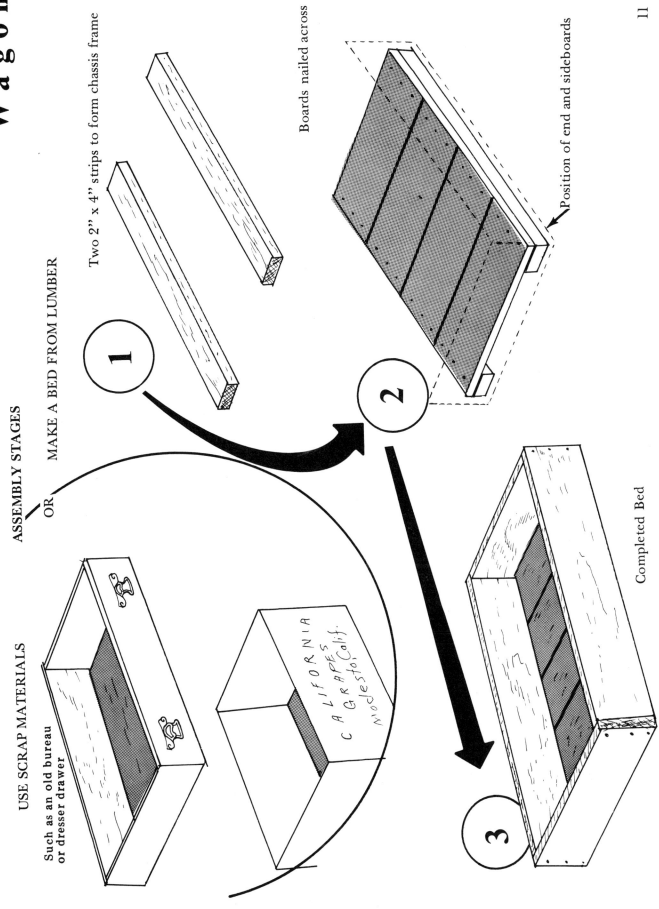

ASSEMBLY STAGES

MAKE A BED FROM LUMBER

Two 2" x 4" strips to form chassis frame

Boards nailed across

Position of end and sideboards

USE SCRAP MATERIALS

Such as an old bureau or dresser drawer

CALIFORNIA
GRAPES
CA
Modesto, Calif.

Completed Bed

1

2

3

OR

ATTACHING REAR AXLE TREE TO BED OF WAGON

SIMPLE WAGON MOUNT

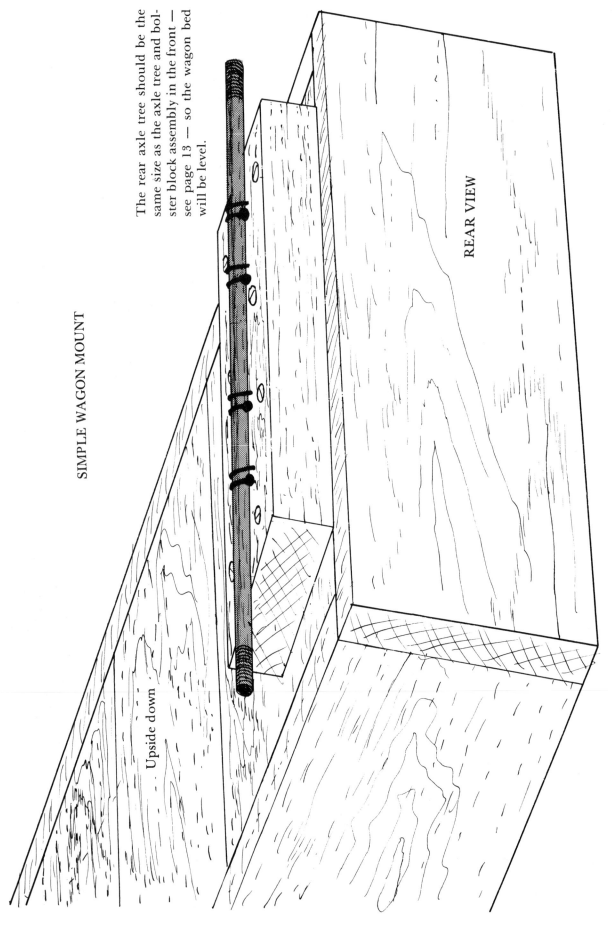

The rear axle tree should be the same size as the axle tree and bolster block assembly in the front — see page 13 — so the wagon bed will be level.

Upside down

REAR VIEW

WAGON FRONT ASSEMBLY

The general size and scale of all vehicles and their parts can be determined by studying the drawings. See page 15

FRONT

Position of wagon tongue

Holes are drilled in all the pieces and in the wagon bottom.

1" x 2" strip

1" x 2" strip

2" x 4" block

Washer

Bolster block

Washer

Nail together

Position of king bolt

AXLE TREE

Lock washer

Nut

See page 15 for handle and tongue assembly

13

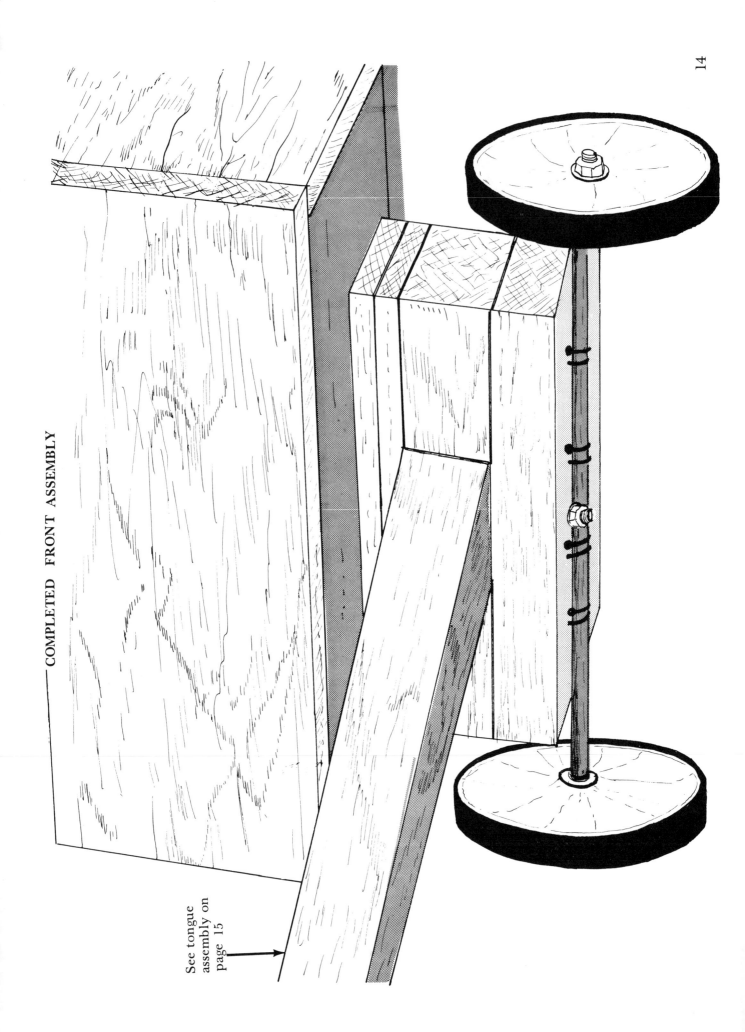

COMPLETED FRONT ASSEMBLY

See tongue
assembly on
page 15

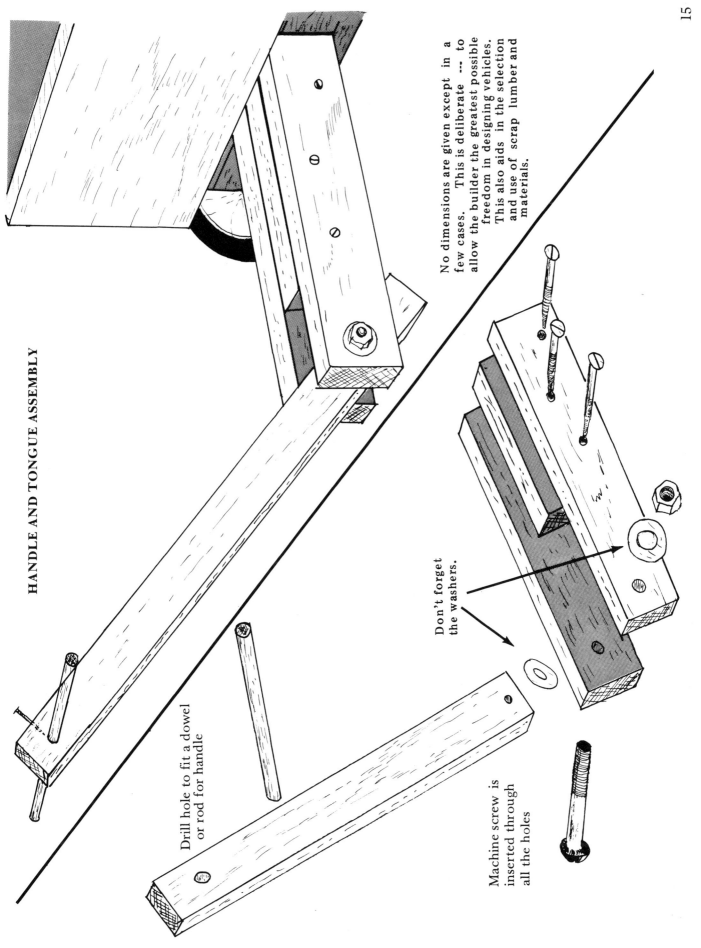

HANDLE AND TONGUE ASSEMBLY

No dimensions are given except in a few cases. This is deliberate -- to allow the builder the greatest possible freedom in designing vehicles. This also aids in the selection and use of scrap lumber and materials.

Don't forget the washers.

Drill hole to fit a dowel or rod for handle

Machine screw is inserted through all the holes

15

Wagon

WAGON WITH ROPE INSTEAD OF TONGUE AND HANDLE

STEERING BY ROPE

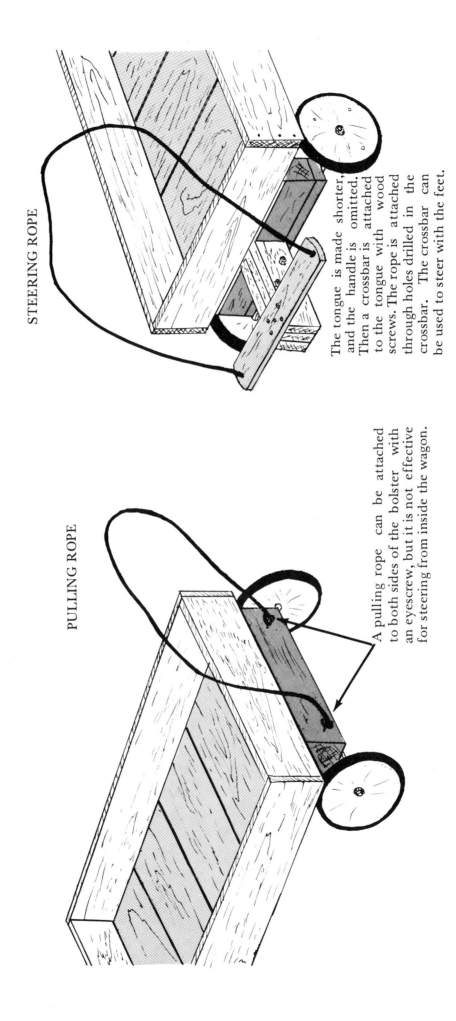

STEERING ROPE

The tongue is made shorter, and the handle is omitted. Then a crossbar is attached to the tongue with wood screws. The rope is attached through holes drilled in the crossbar. The crossbar can be used to steer with the feet.

PULLING ROPE

A pulling rope can be attached to both sides of the bolster with an eyescrew, but it is not effective for steering from inside the wagon.

Skateboard

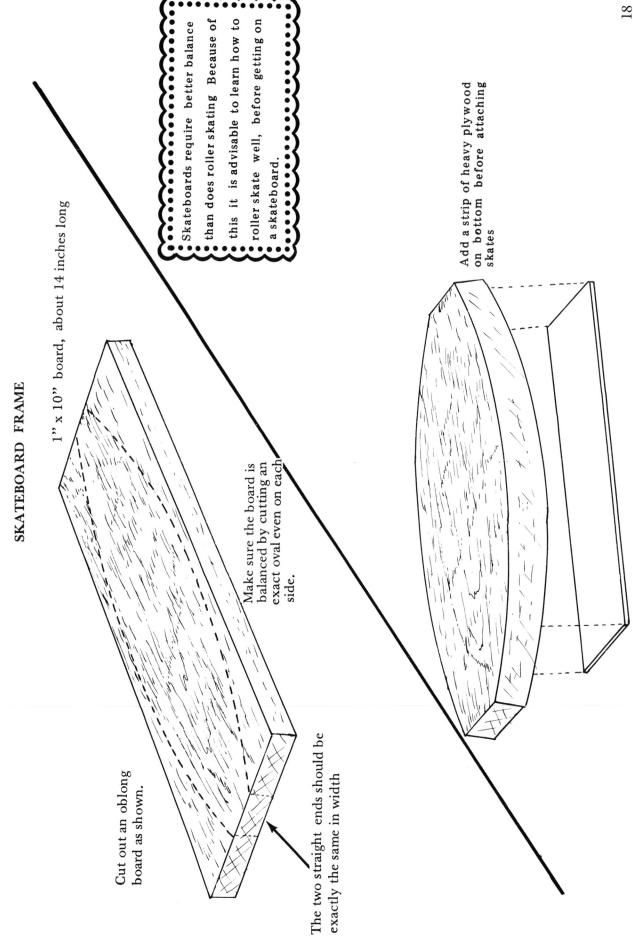

Skateboards require better balance than does roller skating. Because of this it is advisable to learn how to roller skate well, before getting on a skateboard.

SKATEBOARD FRAME

1" x 10" board, about 14 inches long

Make sure the board is balanced by cutting an exact oval even on each side.

Cut out an oblong board as shown.

The two straight ends should be exactly the same in width

Add a strip of heavy plywood on bottom before attaching skates

ADDING SKATES

BOARD SHOWN UPSIDE DOWN

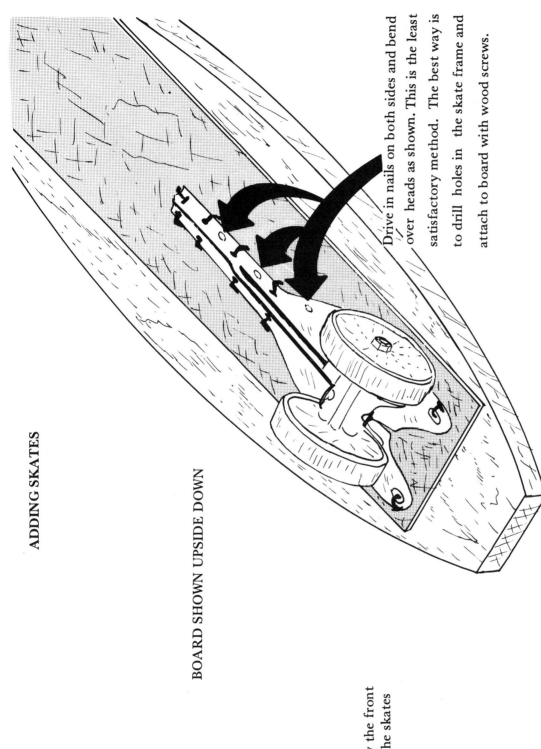

Drive in nails on both sides and bend over heads as shown. This is the least satisfactory method. The best way is to drill holes in the skate frame and attach to board with wood screws.

Use only the front part of the skates

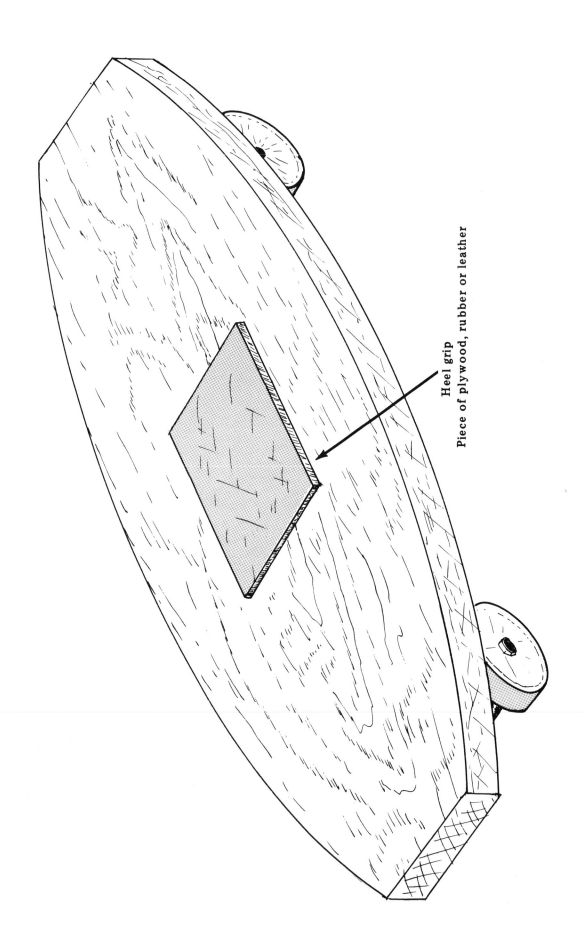

Skateboard

Heel grip
Piece of plywood, rubber or leather

Skate Scooter

MATERIALS

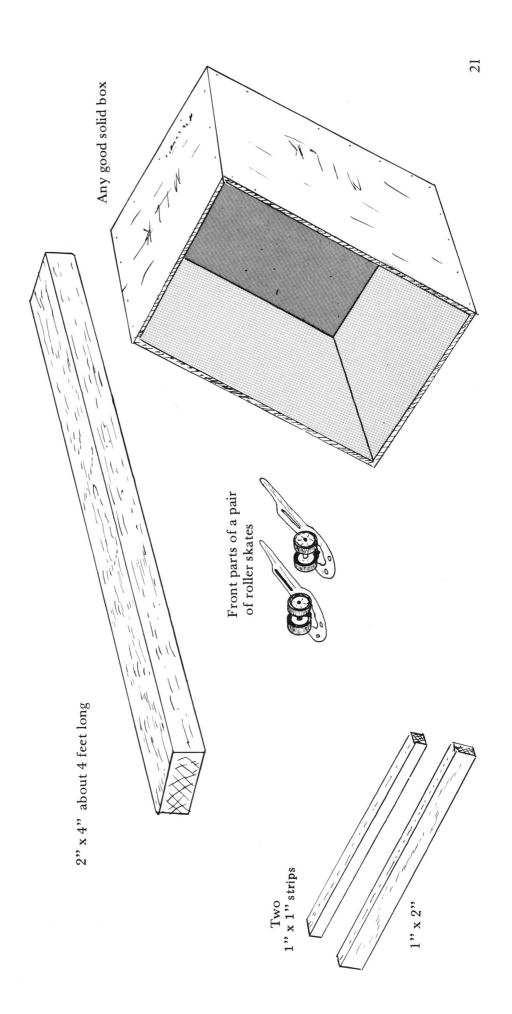

Any good solid box

2" x 4" about 4 feet long

Front parts of a pair
of roller skates

Two
1" x 1" strips

1" x 2"

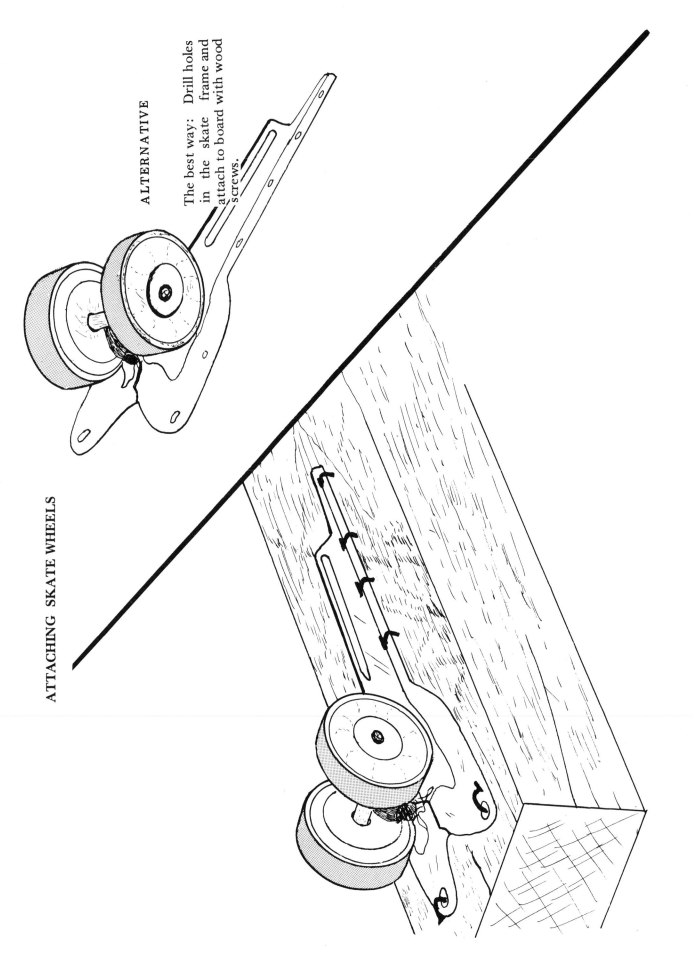

ATTACHING SKATE WHEELS

ALTERNATIVE

The best way: Drill holes in the skate frame and attach to board with wood screws.

22

ATTACHING BOX AND STAND

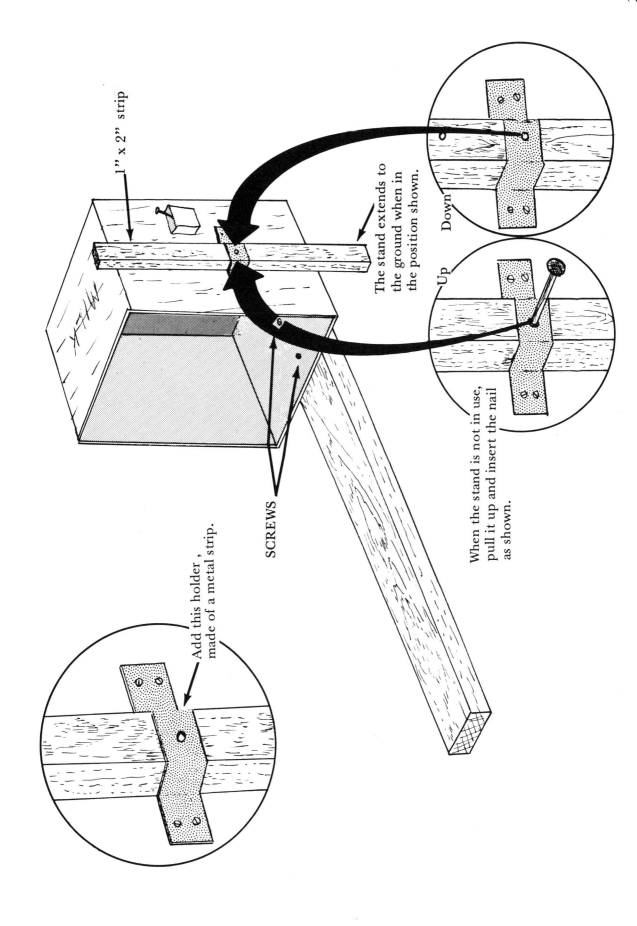

1" x 2" strip

Add this holder, made of a metal strip.

SCREWS

The stand extends to the ground when in the position shown.

Up   Down

When the stand is not in use, pull it up and insert the nail as shown.

ASSEMBLY

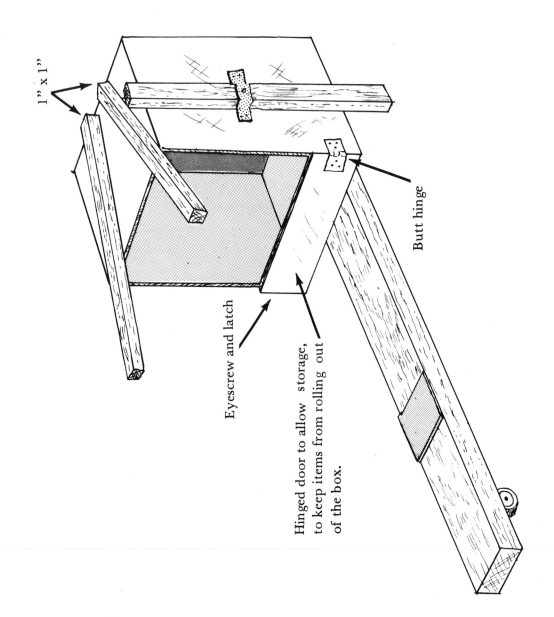

1" x 1"

Butt hinge

Eyescrew and latch

Hinged door to allow storage,
to keep items from rolling out
of the box.

Skate scooter

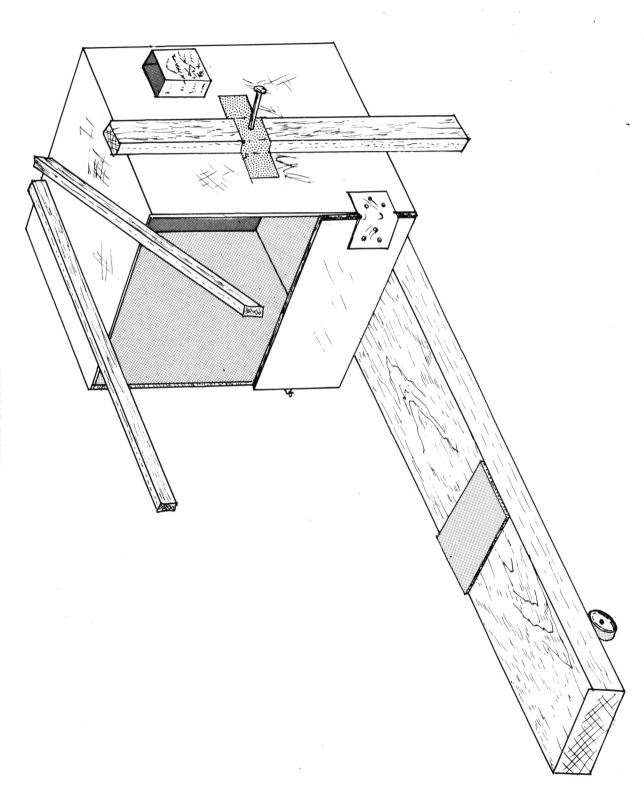

The Mainliner (racer)

BASIC FRAMEWORK

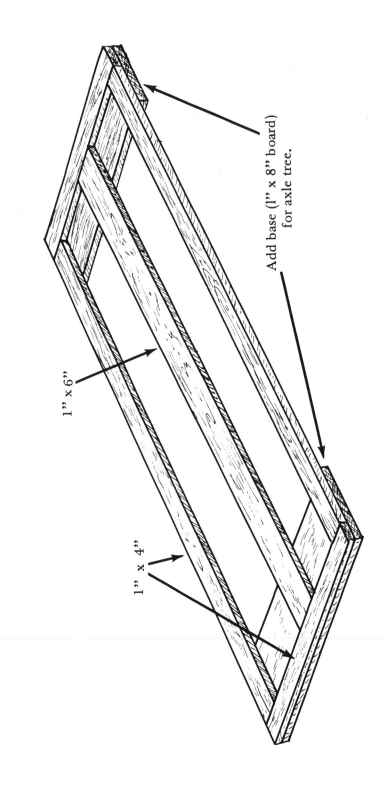

1" x 6"

1" x 4"

Add base (1" x 8" board) for axle tree.

Choose only the lightest weight materials

AXLE TREES

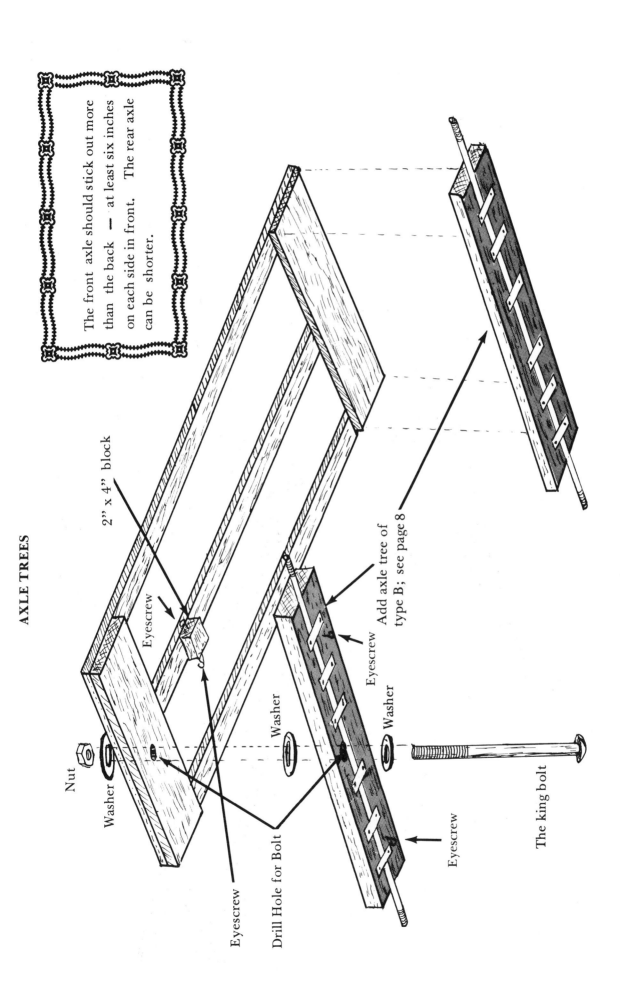

The front axle should stick out more than the back — at least six inches on each side in front. The rear axle can be shorter.

2" x 4" block

Eyescrew

Nut

Washer

Eyescrew

Drill Hole for Bolt

Washer

Eyescrew

Washer

Add axle tree of type B; see page 8

Eyescrew

The king bolt

POWER STEERING ASSEMBLY

The box will become the hood of the racer

Any kind of wheel

See page 75

Washer

Washer

Chassis Top View

Broomhandle or mop handle (steering column)

Steering column hole

See page 64

Axle tree

Steering cable

Eyescrews

The steering cable goes up to the steering column. The cable can be any kind of rope, but not string or twine. They are not strong enough.

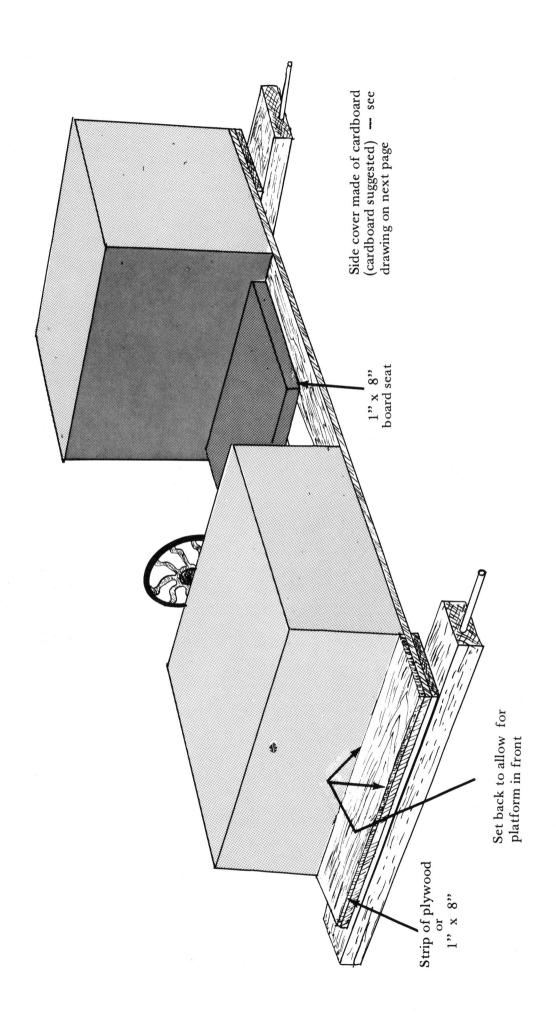

ASSEMBLY

Side cover made of cardboard (cardboard suggested) — see drawing on next page

1" x 8" board seat

Strip of plywood or 1" x 8"

Set back to allow for platform in front

The Mainliner racer

Two-Wheel
Footboard Scooter

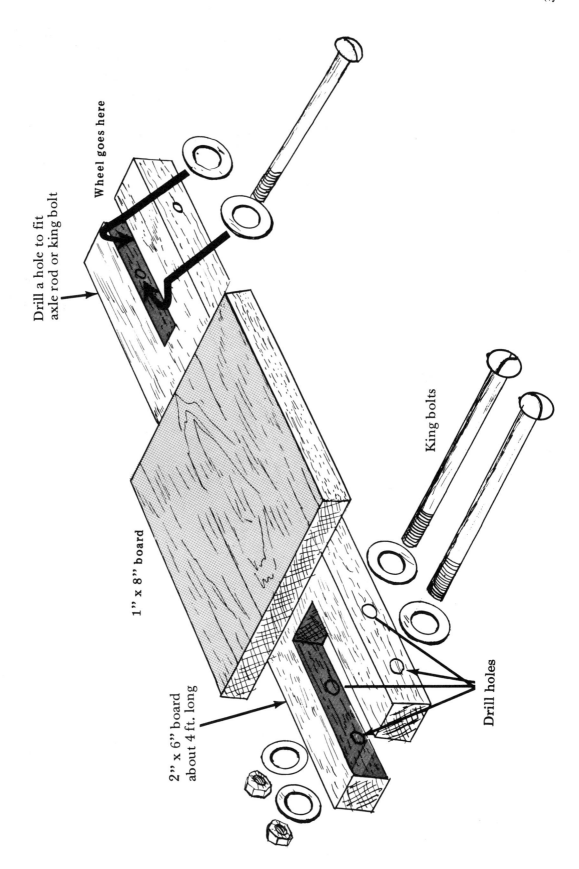

FOOTBOARD AND FRAME

Wheel goes here

Drill a hole to fit
axle rod or king bolt

1" x 8" board

King bolts

2" x 6" board
about 4 ft. long

Drill holes

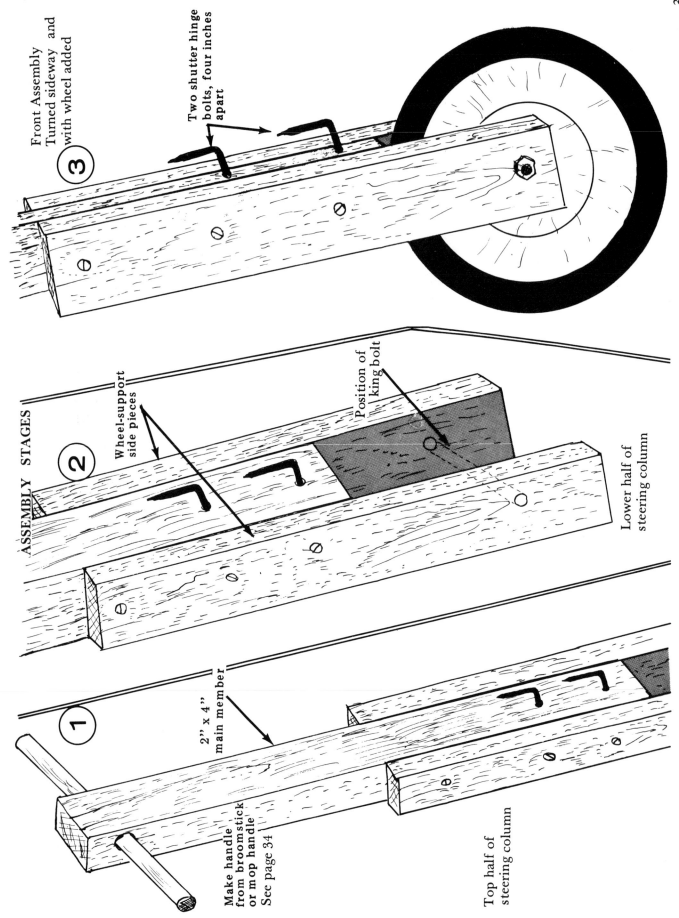

Front Assembly
Turned sideway and
with wheel added

③

Two shutter hinge
bolts, four inches
apart

ASSEMBLY STAGES

②

Wheel-support
side pieces

Position of
king bolt

Lower half of
steering column

①

2'' x 4''
main member

Make handle
from broomstick
or mop handle
See page 34

Top half of
steering column

CONNECTOR ASSEMBLY

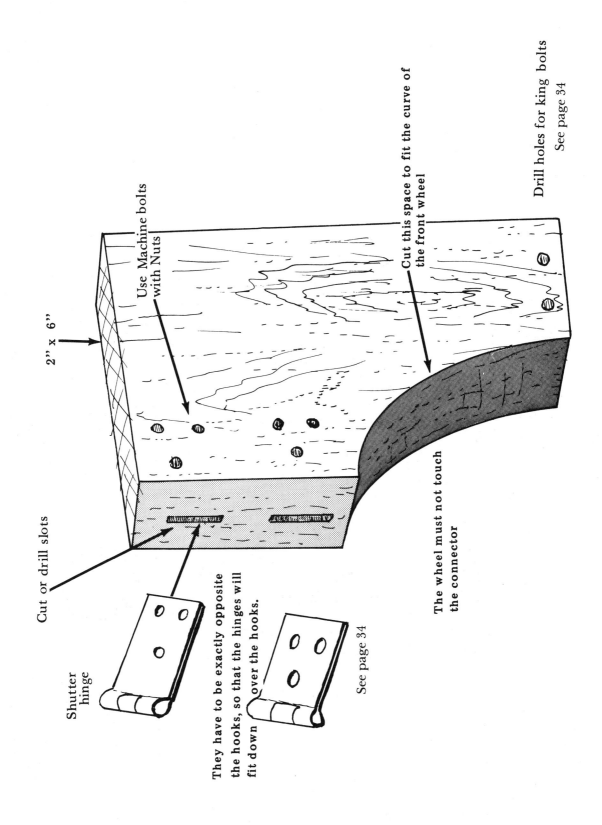

2" x 6"

Use Machine bolts
with Nuts

Cut this space to fit the curve of
the front wheel

Drill holes for king bolts
See page 34

Cut or drill slots

The wheel must not touch
the connector

Shutter
hinge

They have to be exactly opposite
the hooks, so that the hinges will
fit down over the hooks.

See page 34

PUTTING THE SCOOTER TOGETHER

Enlarged lower section of Front Assembly

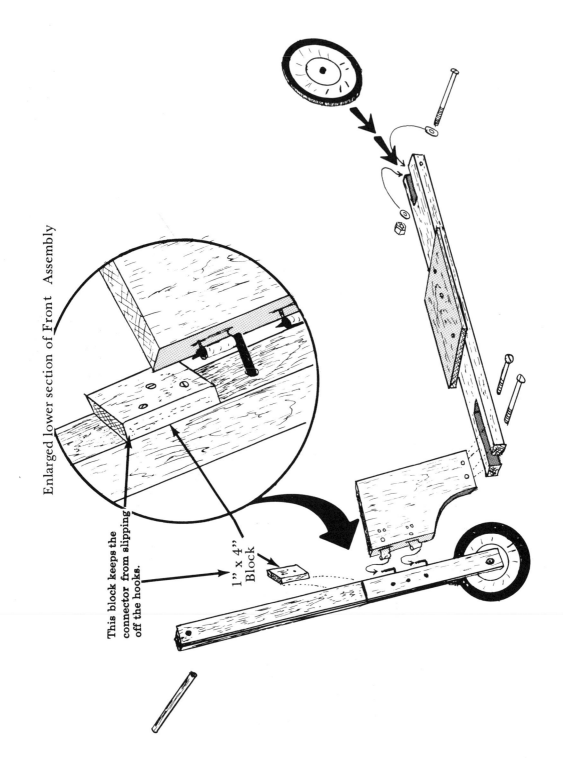

This block keeps the
connector from slipping
off the hooks.

1" x 4"
Block

Two-Wheel Footboard scooter

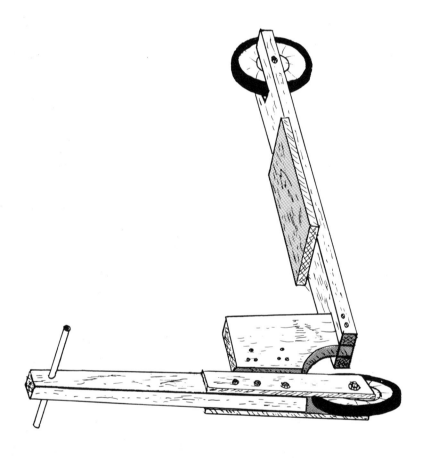

Buckboard (wagon)

BUCKBOARD ASSEMBLY

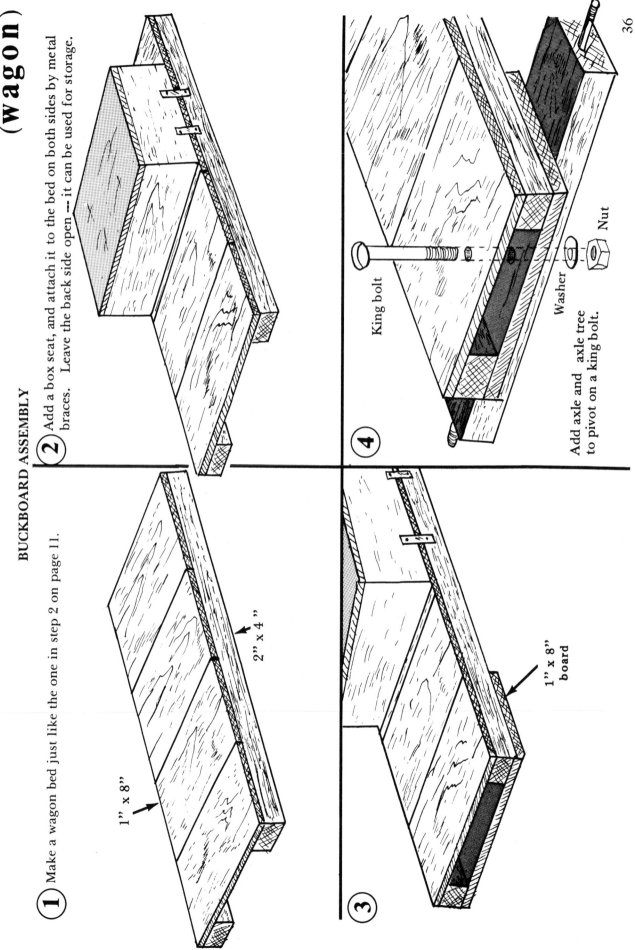

1 Make a wagon bed just like the one in step 2 on page 11.

1" x 8"

2" x 4"

2 Add a box seat, and attach it to the bed on both sides by metal braces. Leave the back side open — it can be used for storage.

3 1" x 8" board

4 Add axle and axle tree to pivot on a king bolt.

King bolt

Washer

Nut

ADDING BUCKBOARD

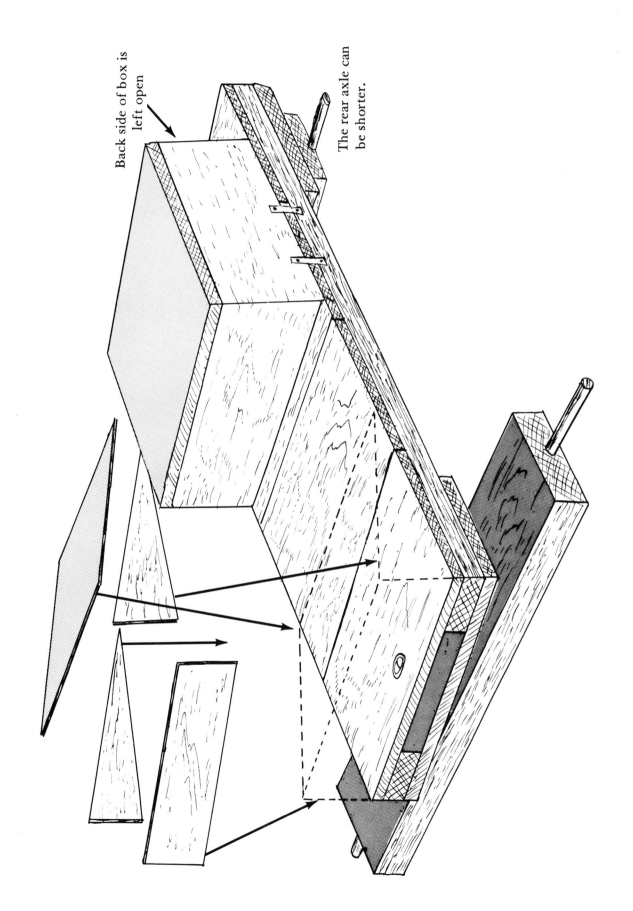

Back side of box is left open

The rear axle can be shorter.

MAKING BRAKES

Brakes can be placed on any wheel, using this same general design, which must include the brake mounted on a pivoting machine screw.

Add nut from inside

2" x 4" block

1" x 2" board

Brake can be added to either side of wagon

Brake block and handle are even (flush) on this side — the side toward the body.

1" block

Piece of rubber or leather

Front of brake

CONSTRUCTING THE REAR SECTION

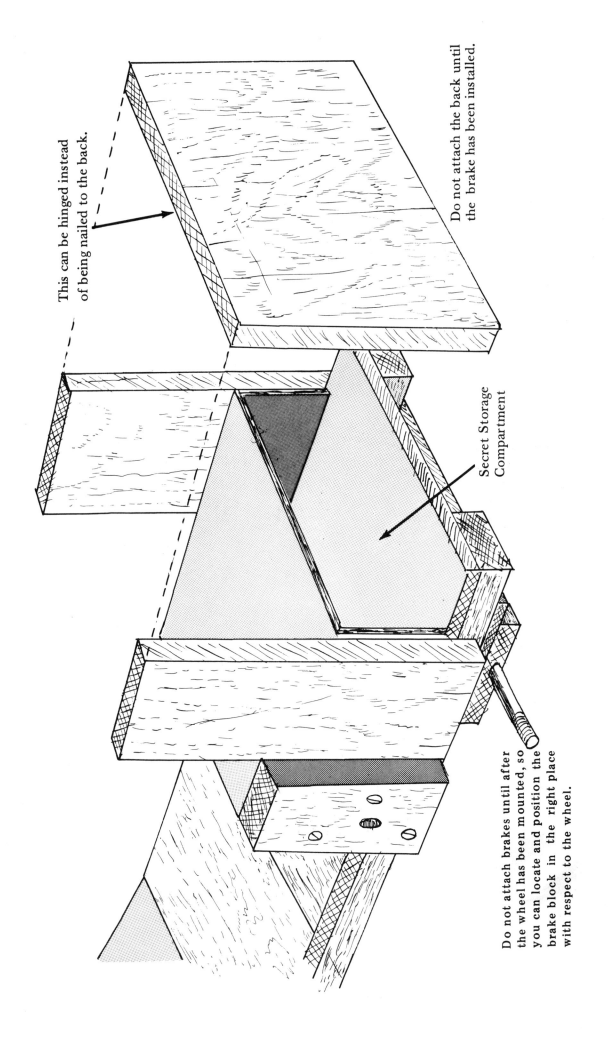

This can be hinged instead of being nailed to the back.

Do not attach the back until the brake has been installed.

Secret Storage Compartment

Do not attach brakes until after the wheel has been mounted, so you can locate and position the brake block in the right place with respect to the wheel.

Buckboard

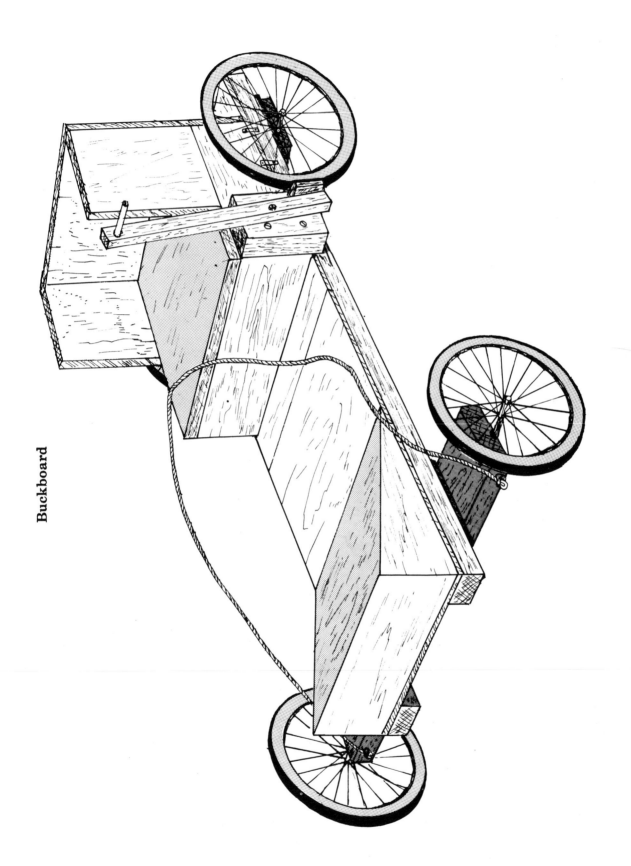

Sport Roadster

CHASSIS FRAMEWORK

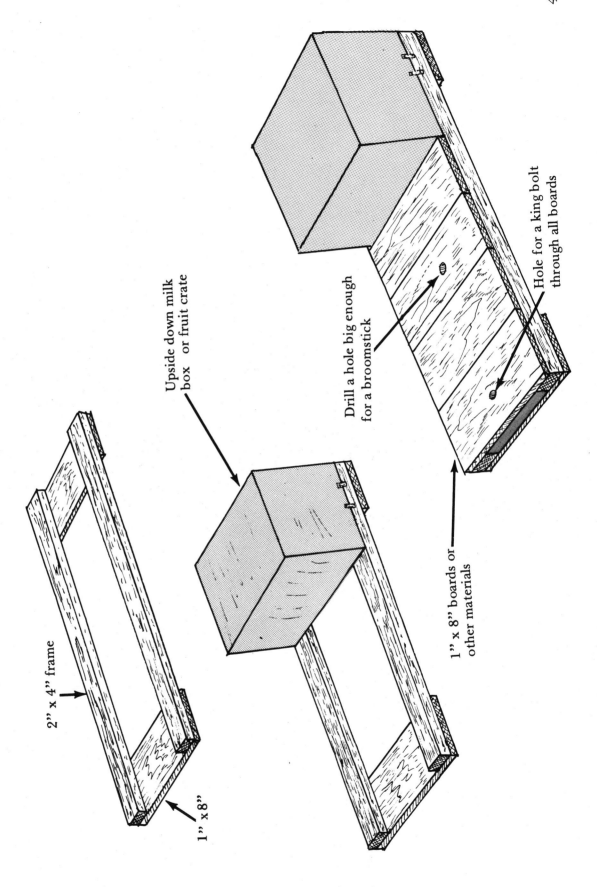

Upside down milk box or fruit crate

2" x 4" frame

1" x 8"

Drill a hole big enough for a broomstick

Hole for a king bolt through all boards

1" x 8" boards or other materials

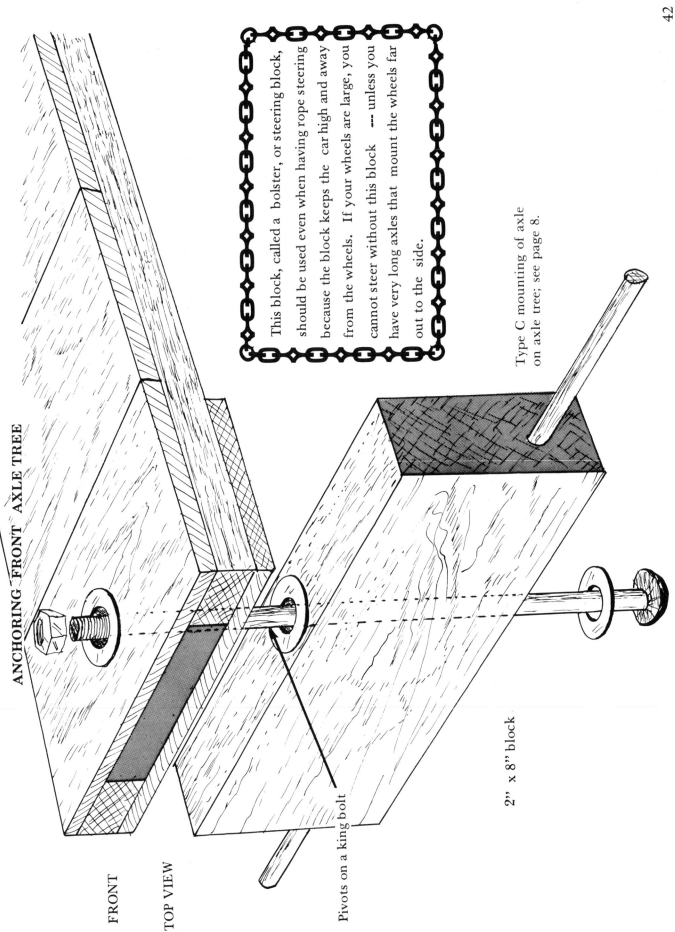

ANCHORING FRONT AXLE TREE

FRONT

TOP VIEW

Pivots on a king bolt

2" x 8" block

This block, called a bolster, or steering block, should be used even when having rope steering because the block keeps the car high and away from the wheels. If your wheels are large, you cannot steer without this block — unless you have very long axles that mount the wheels far out to the side.

Type C mounting of axle on axle tree; see page 8.

BASE FOR STEERING COLUMN

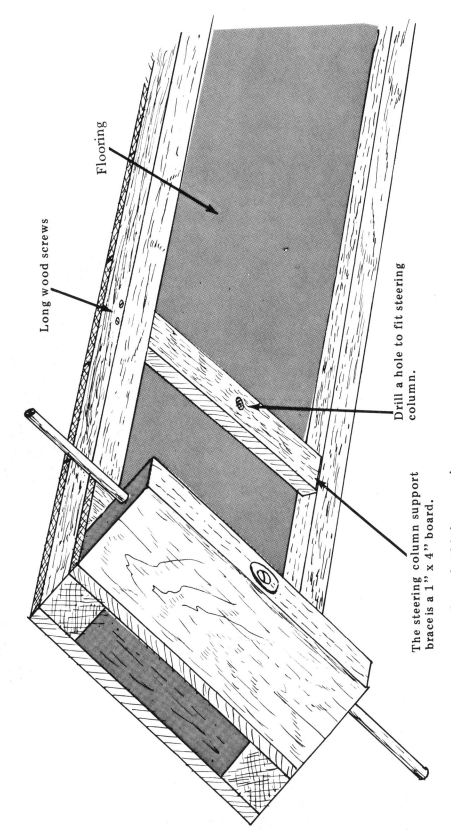

Flooring

Long wood screws

Drill a hole to fit steering column.

The steering column support brace is a 1" x 4" board.

Drill through this brace and straight through the floor.

ADDING STEERING WHEEL AND TOP SUPPORT BRACE

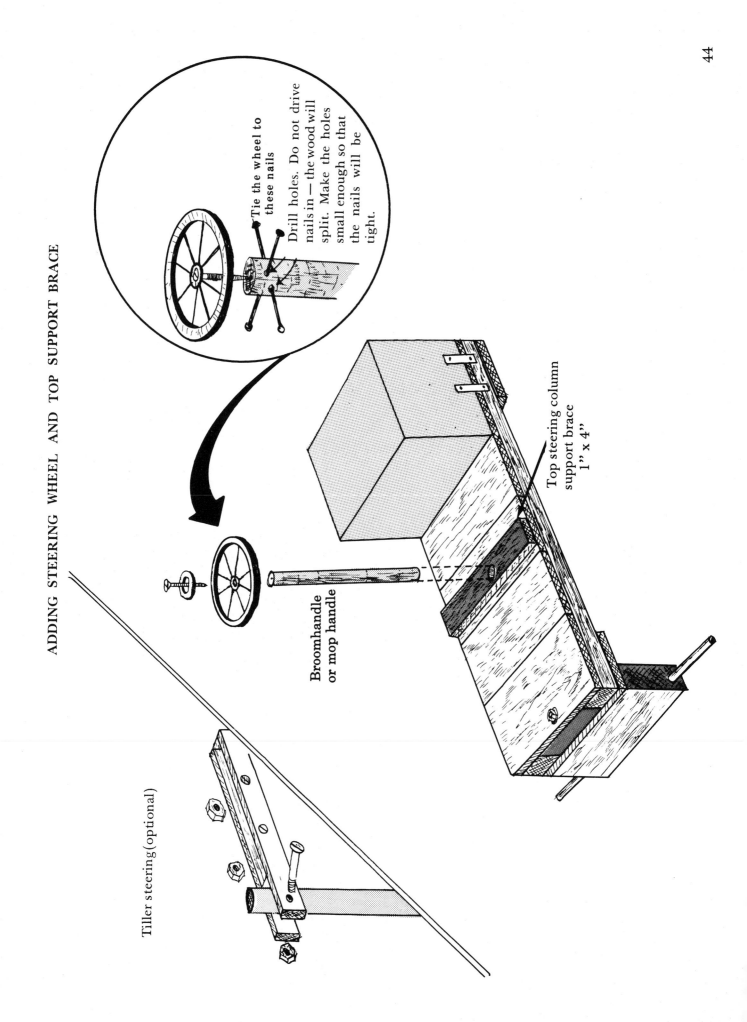

Tie the wheel to these nails

Drill holes. Do not drive nails in — the wood will split. Make the holes small enough so that the nails will be tight.

Broomhandle or mop handle

Top steering column support brace 1" x 4"

Tiller steering(optional)

44

ATTACHING STEERING CABLE TO STEERING COLUMN

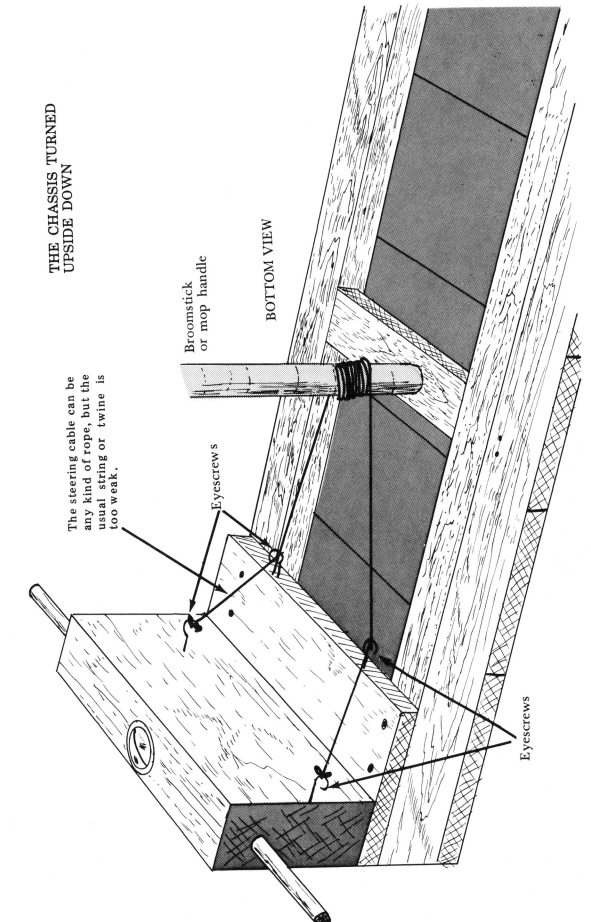

THE CHASSIS TURNED
UPSIDE DOWN

BOTTOM VIEW

Broomstick
or mop handle

Eyescrews

The steering cable can be
any kind of rope, but the
usual string or twine is
too weak.

Eyescrews

45

STEERING AND FRAMEWORK COMPLETED

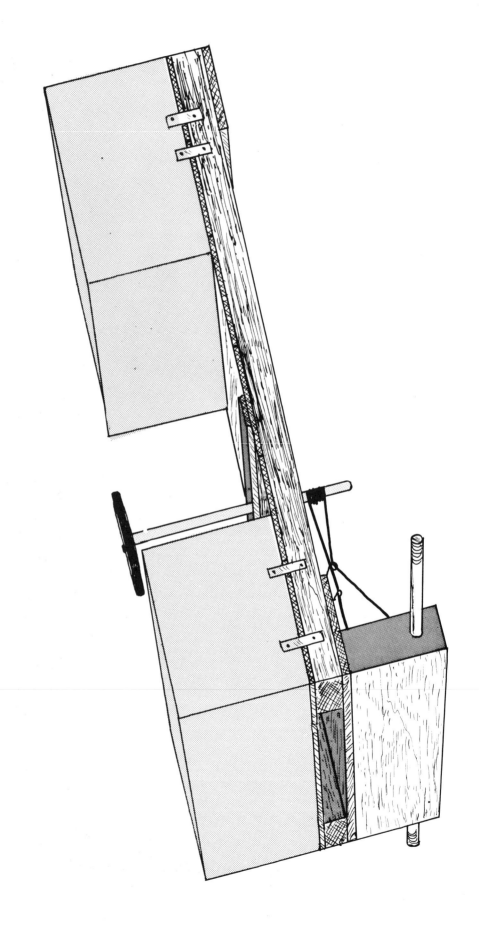

REAR AXLE TREE AND BODY ATTACHMENTS

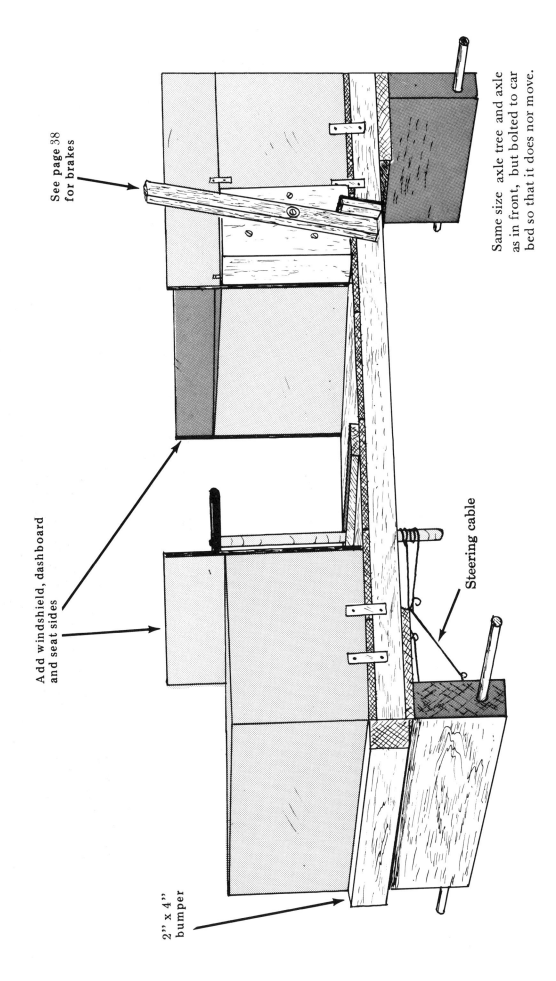

See page 38 for brakes

Add windshield, dashboard and seat sides

2" x 4" bumper

Steering cable

Same size axle tree and axle as in front, but bolted to car bed so that it does nor move.

COMPLETED BODY AND ROOF

Use Scrap Materials

Scrap canvas or oilcloth

1" x 2" crossbeams

1" x 2" roof supports

Shorter than the other supports

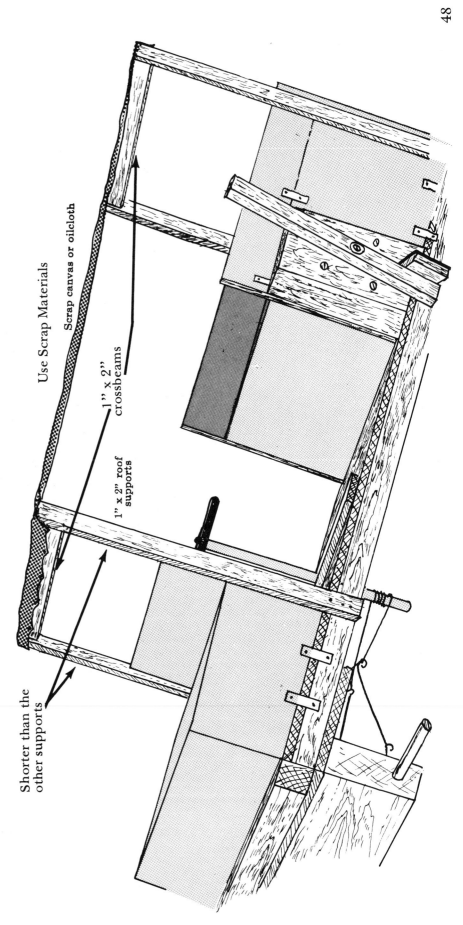

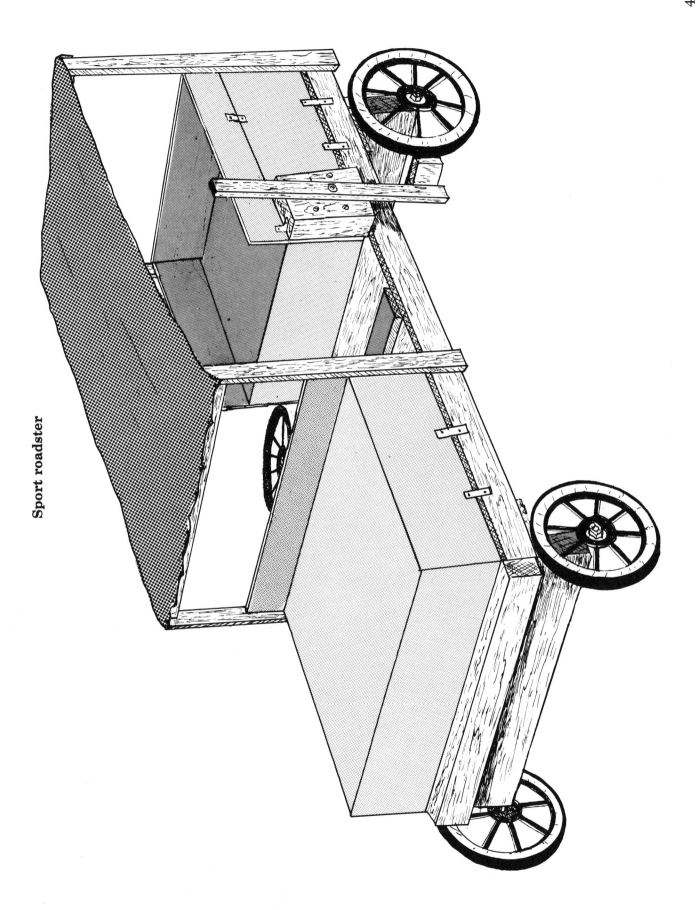

Sport roadster

49

The Whicky-Whack
(carnival whirler)

MATERIALS

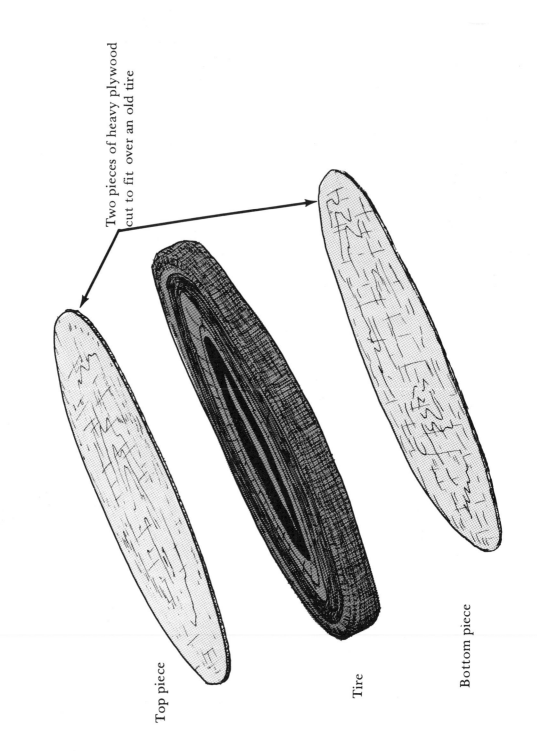

Two pieces of heavy plywood cut to fit over an old tire

Top piece

Tire

Bottom piece

CONSTRUCTING THE WHICKY--WHACK PLATFORM

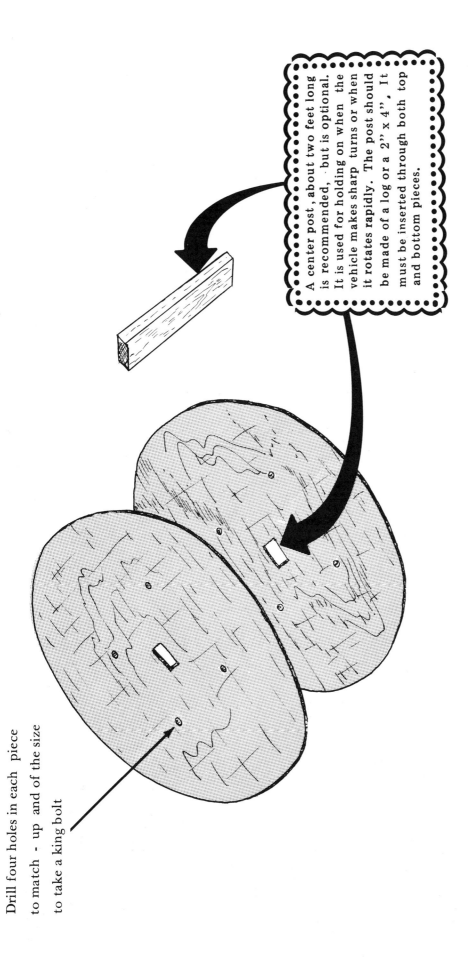

A center post, about two feet long is recommended, but is optional. It is used for holding on when the vehicle makes sharp turns or when it rotates rapidly. The post should be made of a log or a 2'' x 4''. It must be inserted through both top and bottom pieces.

Drill four holes in each piece to match - up and of the size to take a king bolt

Top and Bottom Sections of the Vehicle

GETTING CASTERS FOR THE WHICKY -- WHACK
You need at least three, but four are best

(1) Casters Detached From Furniture

Find an old bureau or other piece of furniture that has casters. Remove the legs or the units to which the legs and casters are attached. The whole caster and unit should be no more than four inches long.

Most casters have barrels about 2½ inches long

Saw off a square section of the leg

Leg of an old swivel desk chair

GETTING CASTERS FOR THE WHICKY - WHACK

PREPARING CASTER BLOCKS

Cut two blocks from 2" x 4" board. Make each block about 4 inches long.

NOTE: You will need 4 pairs of blocks - eight blocks – for the four-caster whicky-whack and three pairs - six blocks - for the three-caster whicky-whack.

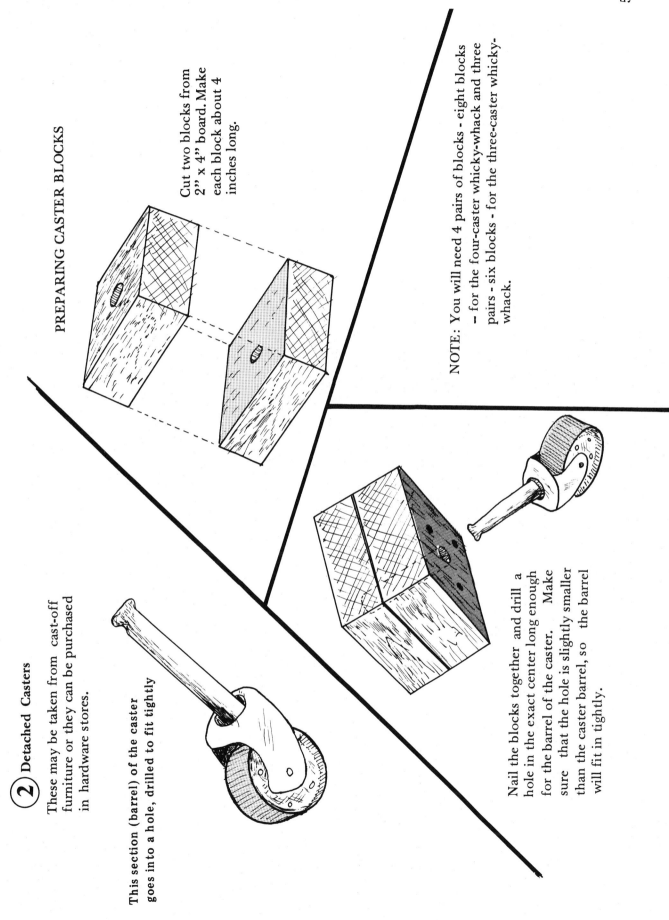

(2) Detached Casters

These may be taken from cast-off furniture or they can be purchased in hardware stores.

This section (barrel) of the caster goes into a hole, drilled to fit tightly

Nail the blocks together and drill a hole in the exact center long enough for the barrel of the caster.   Make sure that the hole is slightly smaller than the caster barrel, so   the barrel will fit in tightly.

LOCATION OF THE CASTER BLOCKS

Location of blocks if you
have only three casters

This type (the three-wheel type)
should not be used if small children
are going to ride the vehicle.

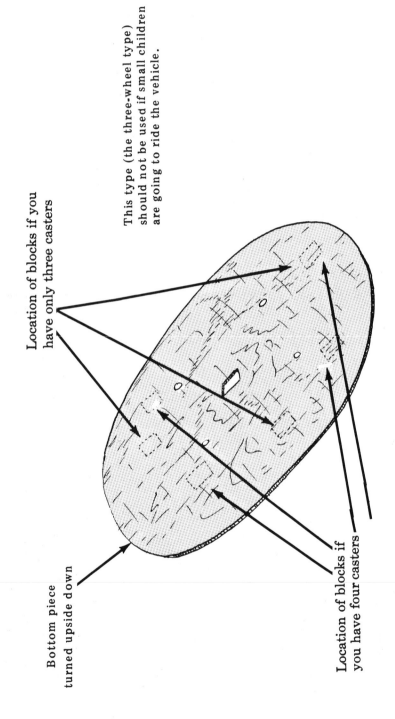

Bottom piece
turned upside down

Location of blocks if
you have four casters

The four-caster whicky-whack is
safer and more manageable.

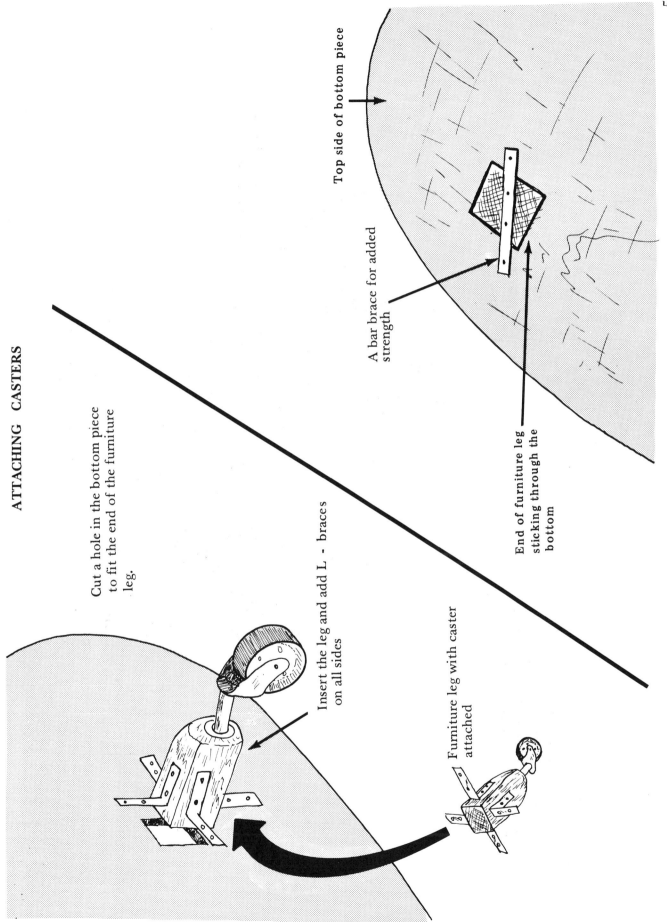

ATTACHING CASTERS

Cut a hole in the bottom piece to fit the end of the furniture leg.

Insert the leg and add L - braces on all sides

Furniture leg with caster attached

Top side of bottom piece

A bar brace for added strength

End of furniture leg sticking through the bottom

CASTERS
Mounted on Blocks

ALTERNATIVE
Have your casters threaded in a machine shop or hardware store. Threaded barrels can be bolted to the bottom.

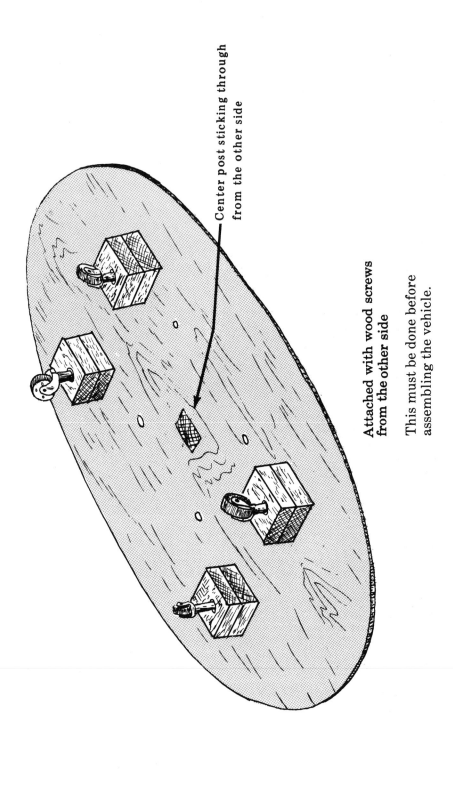

Center post sticking through from the other side

Attached with wood screws from the other side

This must be done before assembling the vehicle.

PUTTING THE WHICKY – WHACK TOGETHER

Use washers on both sides to protect the wood from wear.

King bolts

Washers

Nuts

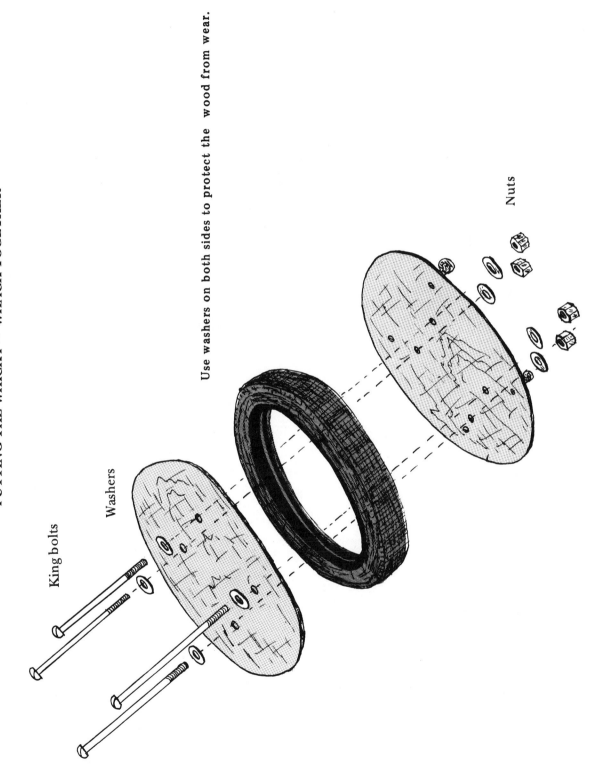

Whicky-Whack carnival whirler

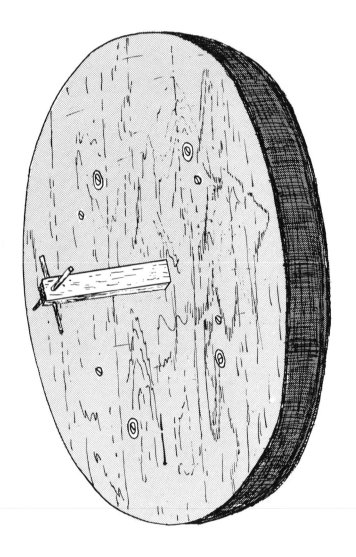

Soapbox Racer

FRAMEWORK

THE CHASSIS TURNED UPSIDE DOWN

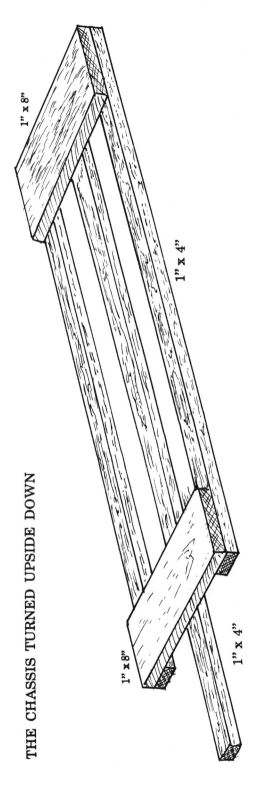

1" x 8"

1" x 4"

1" x 8"

1" x 4"

Lightweight frame chassis, constructed of 1" x 4" boards, if possible

FRAMEWORK OF FRONT END

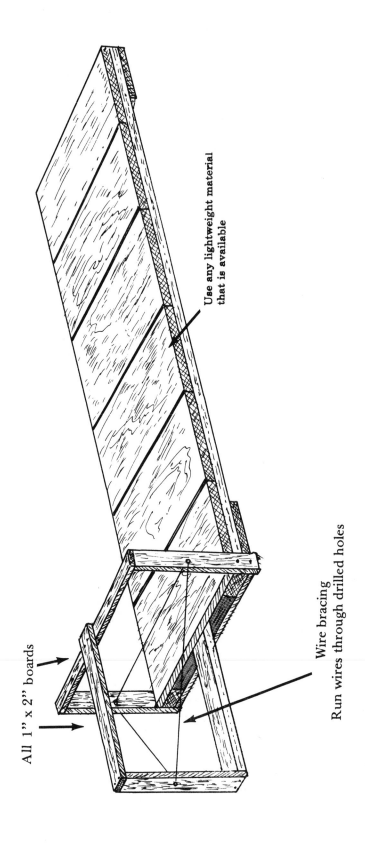

Use any lightweight material that is available

All 1" x 2" boards

Wire bracing
Run wires through drilled holes

AXLE TREES

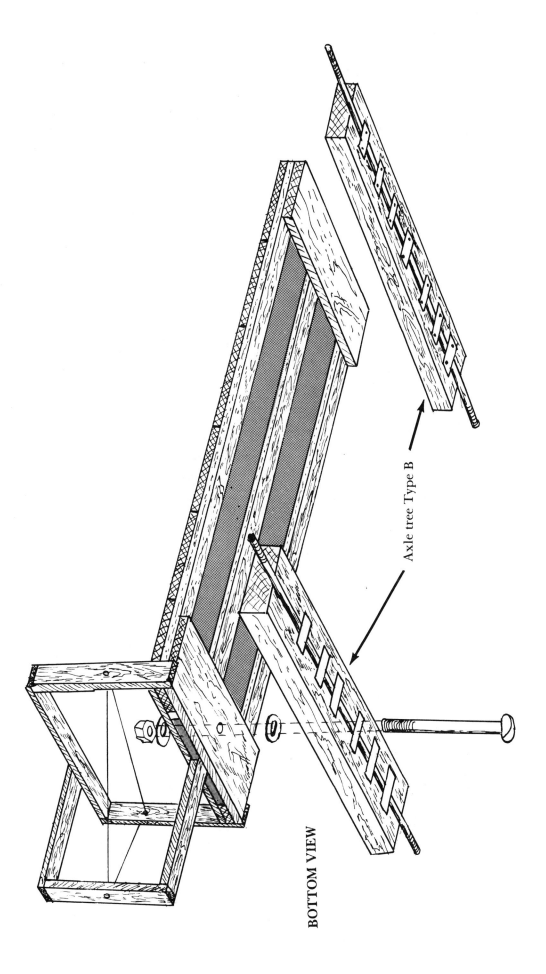

Axle tree Type B

BOTTOM VIEW

ATTACHING STEERING CABLE TO AXLE TREE

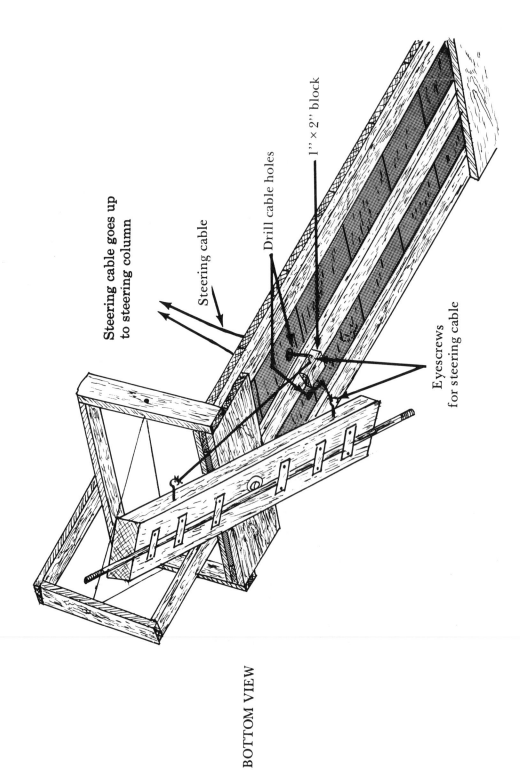

Steering cable goes up
to steering column

Steering cable

Drill cable holes

1" × 2" block

Eyescrews
for steering cable

BOTTOM VIEW

FRAME AND STEERING MECHANISM

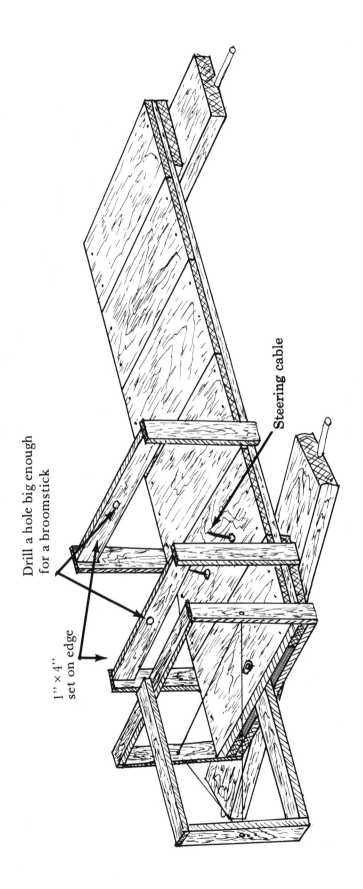

Drill a hole big enough
for a broomstick

1" × 4"
set on edge

Steering cable

STEERING MECHANISM

Make two or three turns around the column, and then put the cable in the hole and pull it tight. Then tie the end so that it will not slip through the hole.

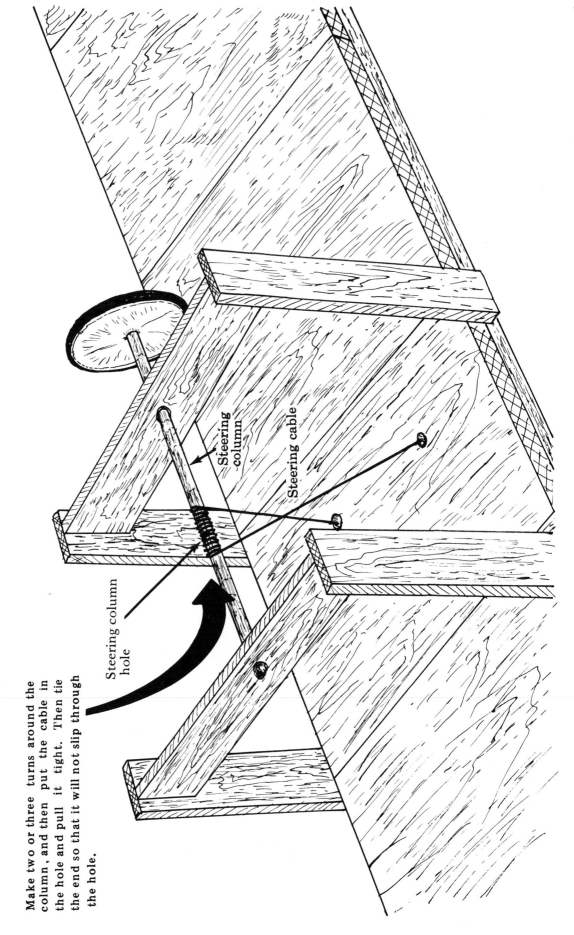

Steering column hole

Steering column

Steering cable

FRAMEWORK AND FLOORING COMPLETED

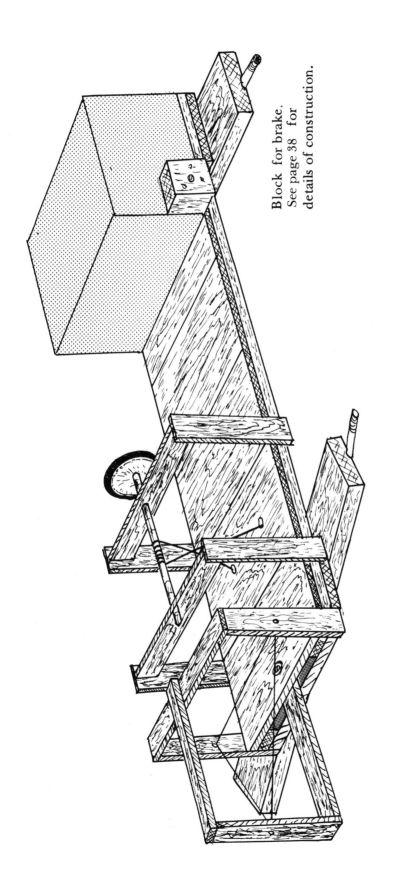

Block for brake.
See page 38 for
details of construction.

COVERING

Pieces of plywood, cardboard or lumber, cut and shaped to desired form

Soapbox racer

Pedal-Powered Raceabout

THE CHASSIS

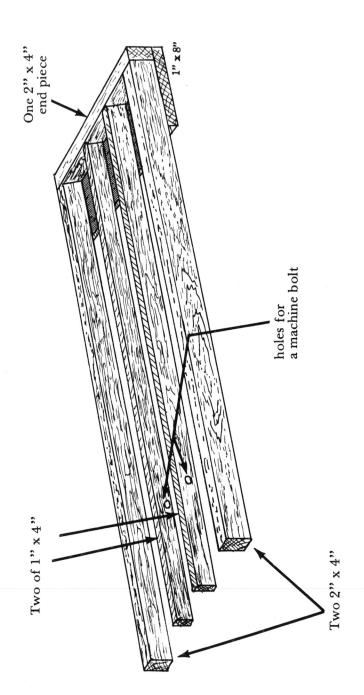

One 2" x 4" end piece

1" x 8"

holes for a machine bolt

Two of 1" x 4"

Two 2" x 4"

PREPARING FOR AXLE TREES AND WORKING PARTS

THE CHASSIS TURNED UPSIDE DOWN

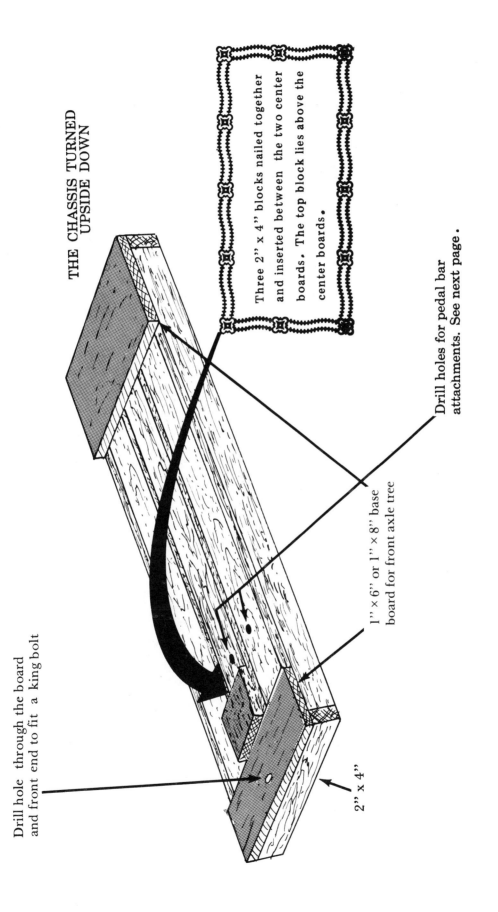

Three 2" x 4" blocks nailed together and inserted between the two center boards. The top block lies above the center boards.

Drill holes for pedal bar attachments. See next page.

1" × 6" or 1" × 8" base board for front axle tree

Drill hole through the board and front end to fit a king bolt

2" x 4"

REAR AXLE AND PEDALS

BACK

Front Axle Mounting is by axle tree bolster board of Type C. See page 8. But the axle must be attached to a high bolster board. The wheels should turn under the vehicle.

Drill holes at the ends as shown here.

The pedal bars are 1" x 2", bolted midway from the ends. They are bolted to the two center boards as shown. Use washers; they must be loose enough to rock back and forth.

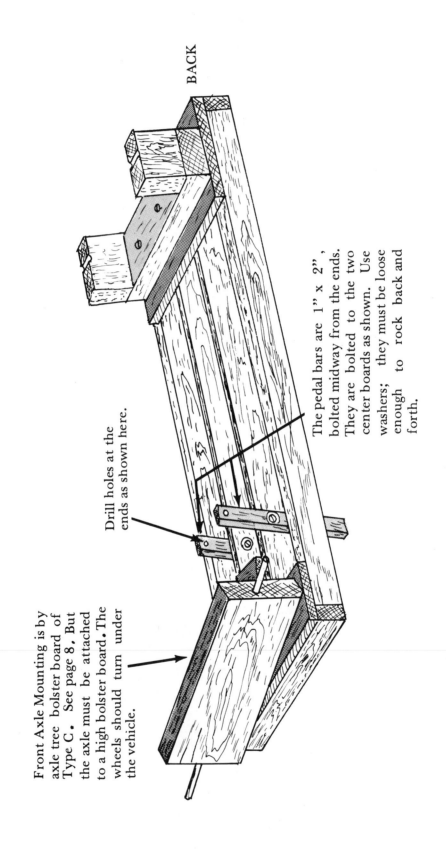

70

PEDAL BARS AND CONNECTING RODS

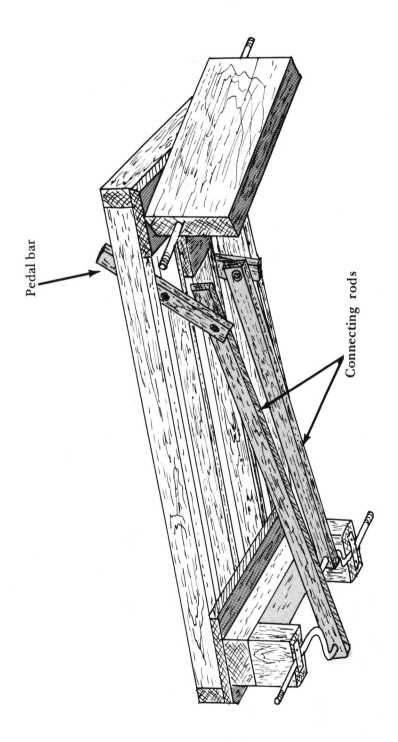

Pedal bar

Connecting rods

ATTACHING STEERING CABLES

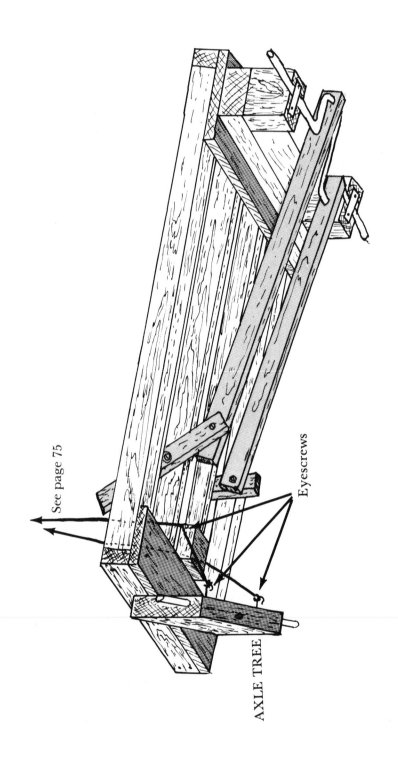

See page 75

Eyescrews

AXLE TREE

COMPLETING REAR DECK WITH SEAT AND COVER

TOP VIEW

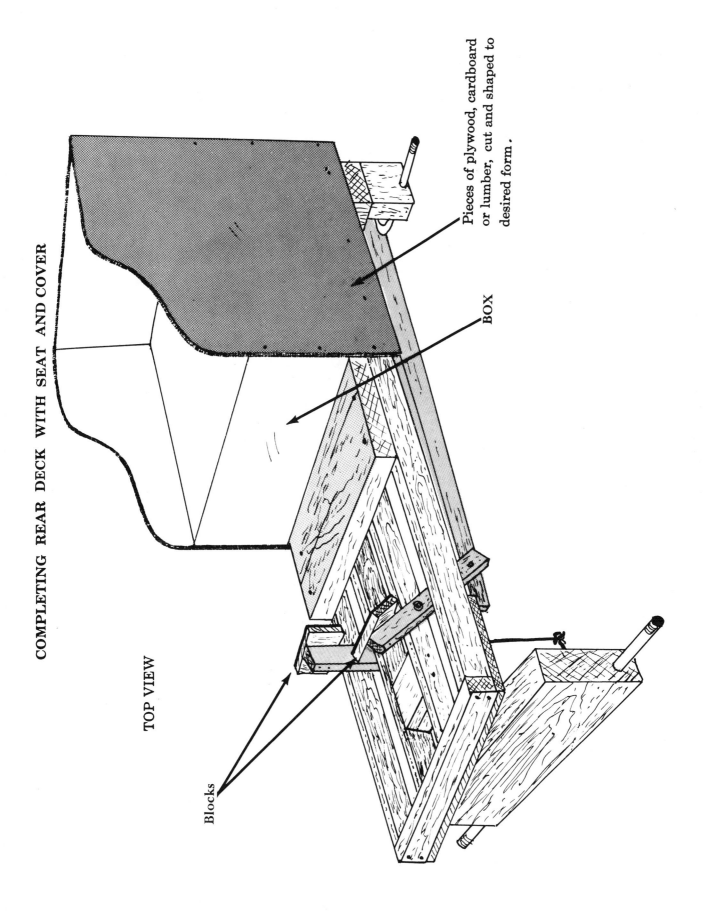

Blocks

BOX

Pieces of plywood, cardboard or lumber, cut and shaped to desired form.

STEERING COLUMN ATTACHMENT FRAME

Make a deep groove with a file or rasp, big enough to fit a broomhandle.

The top piece is shorter, and will be the base for attaching the steering column

Three 2" x 4" pieces nailed together

FRONT ASSEMBLY

2" x 4" support post

Add this brace

Steering cable

The unit will be used to support the steering column and steering wheel.

ATTACHING STEERING COLUMN AND CABLE

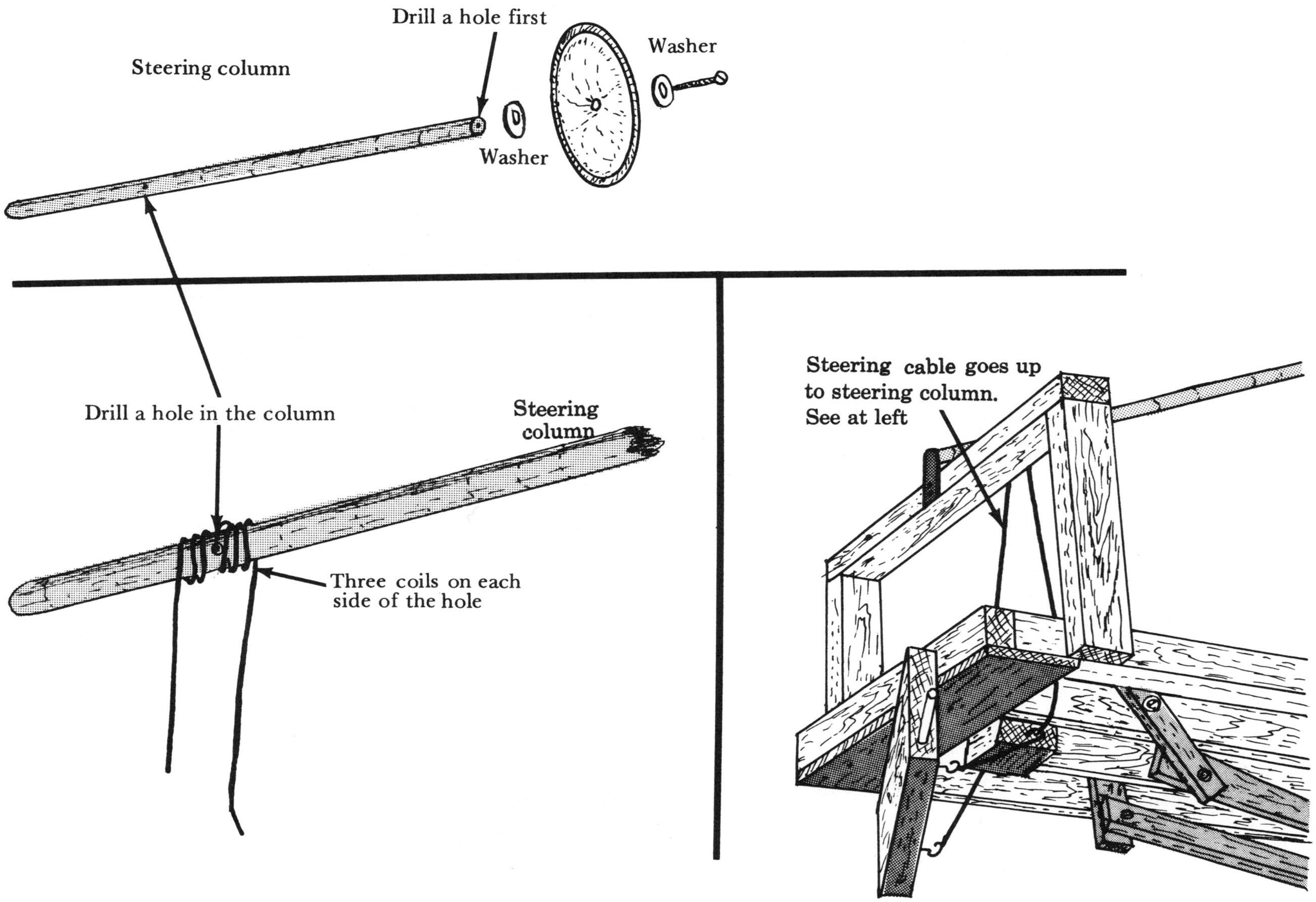

Washer

Drill a hole first

Washer

Steering column

Steering cable goes up to steering column. See at left

Steering column

Three coils on each side of the hole

Drill a hole in the column

75

STEERING COLUMN AND WHEEL IN POSITION

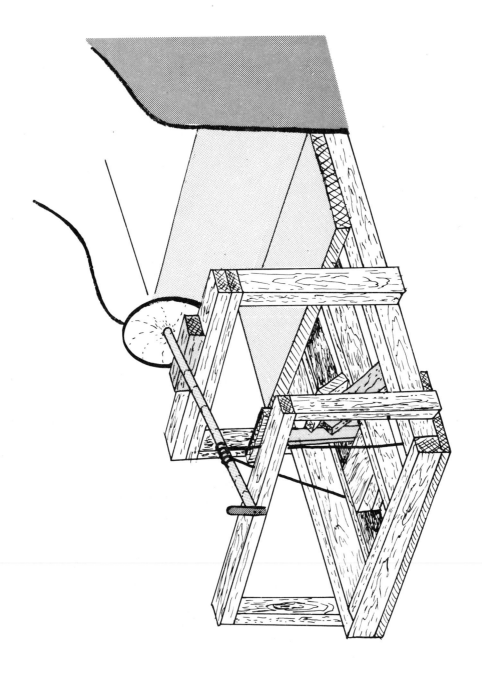

ADDING A HOOD

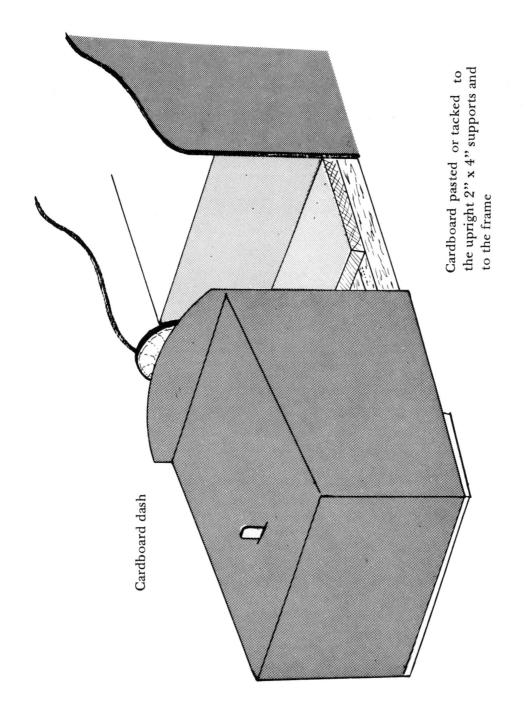

Cardboard dash

Cardboard pasted or tacked to the upright 2" x 4" supports and to the frame

77

Pedal-Powered raceabout

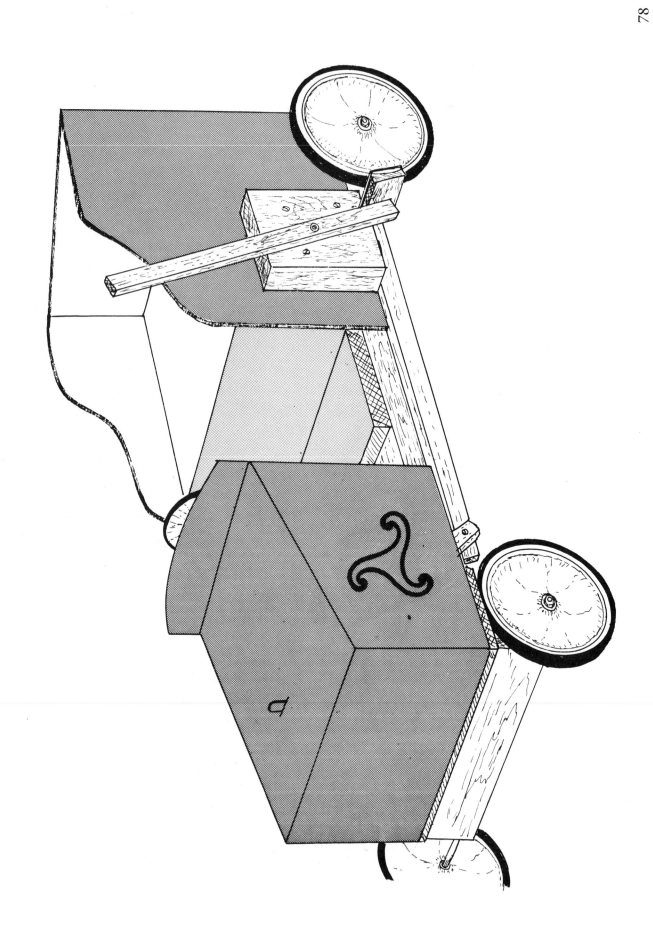

Two-Man Sidewalk Handcar

MAKING THE CHASSIS

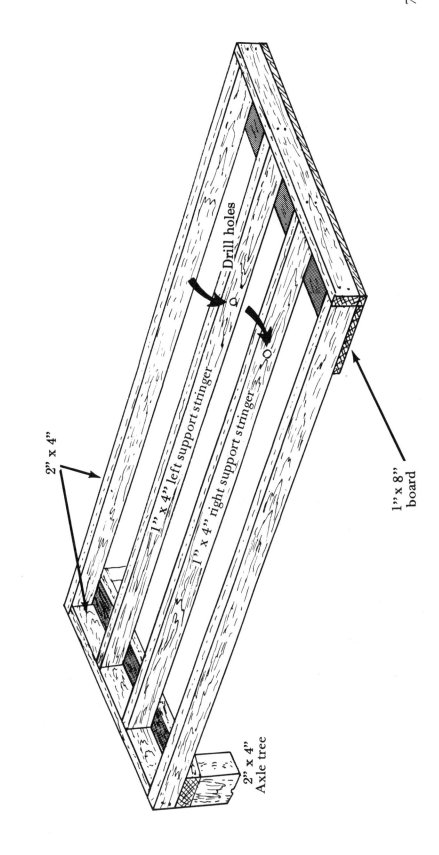

2" x 4"

Drill holes

1" x 4" left support stringer

1" x 4" right support stringer

1" x 8" board

2" x 4" Axle tree

REAR AXLE AND CONNECTING BAR

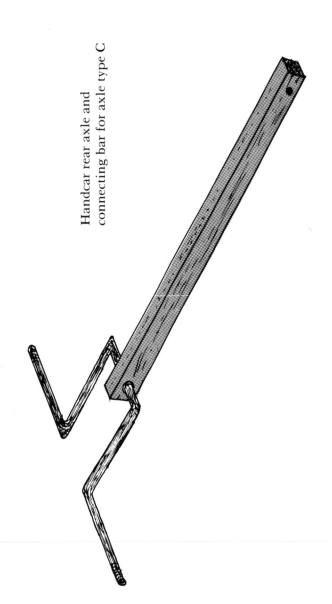

Handcar rear axle and
connecting bar for axle type C

HANDLE BAR AND CONNECTIONS

HANDLE BAR IS LIKE THE ONE MADE FOR THE SCOOTER. SEE PAGE 32

Handle is attached between the stringers with a bolt

Connecting bar (see page 80) **will be attached here. See** page 82

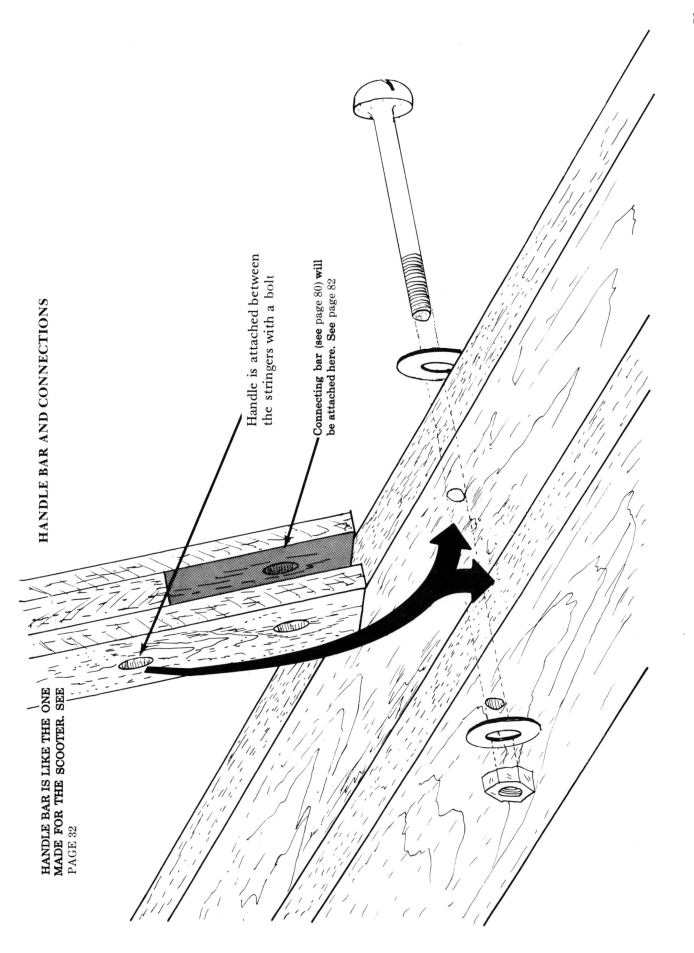

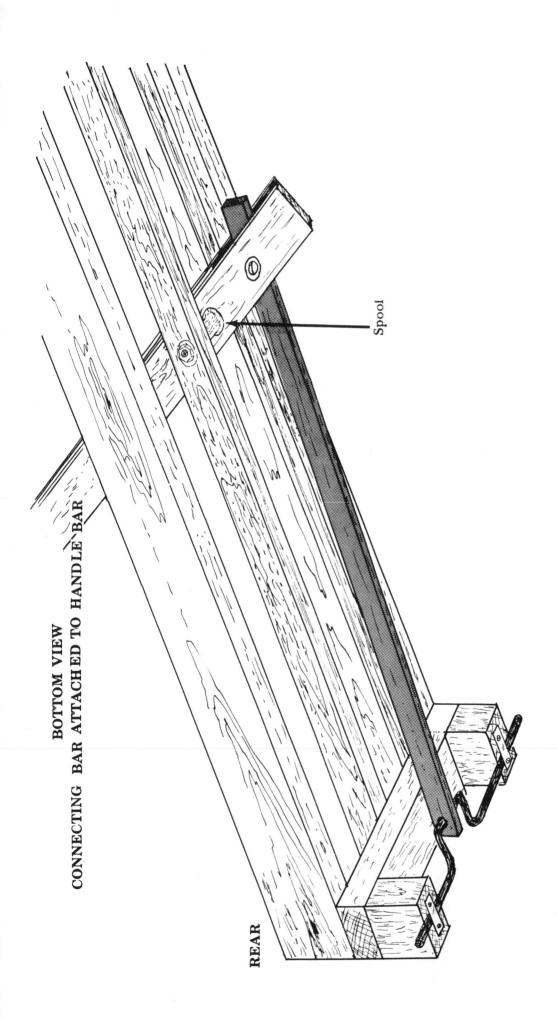

BOTTOM VIEW

CONNECTING BAR ATTACHED TO HANDLE BAR

REAR

Spool

82

HANDLE BAR

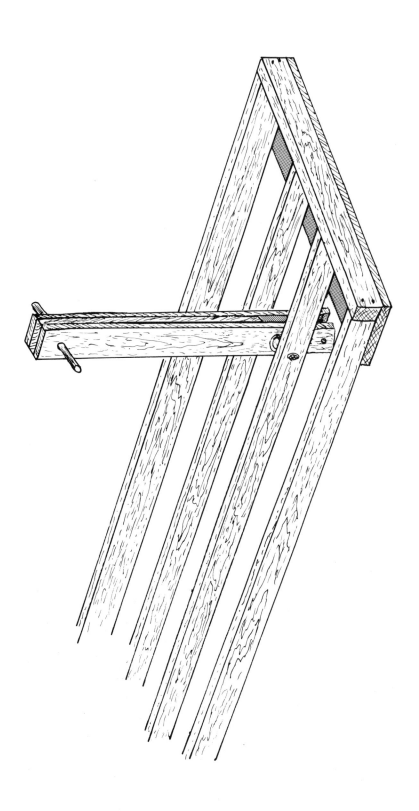

PREPARING BASE FOR STEERING COLUMN

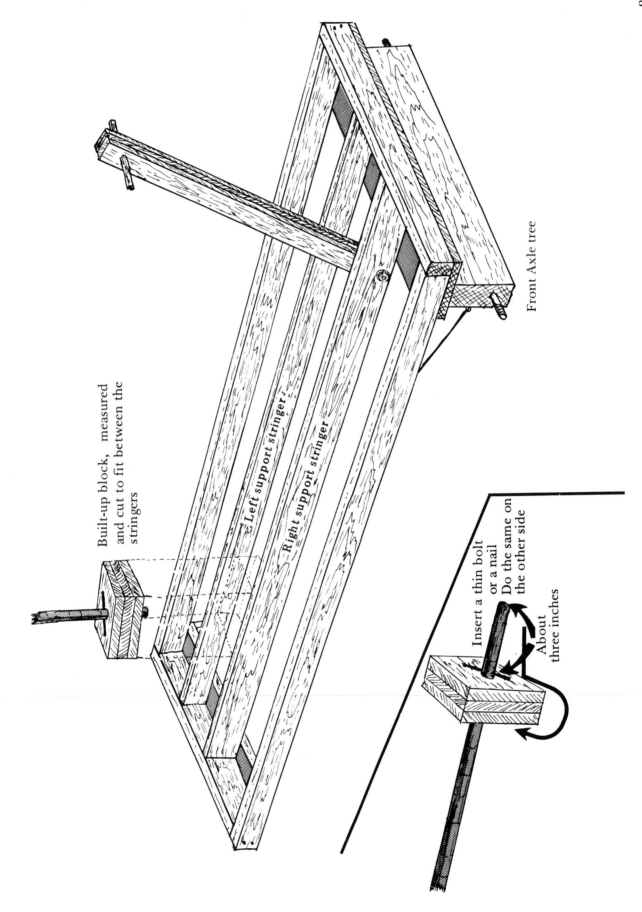

Front Axle tree

Built-up block, measured and cut to fit between the stringers

Left support stringer

Right support stringer

Insert a thin bolt or a nail
Do the same on the other side

About three inches

ATTACHING STEERING CABLES

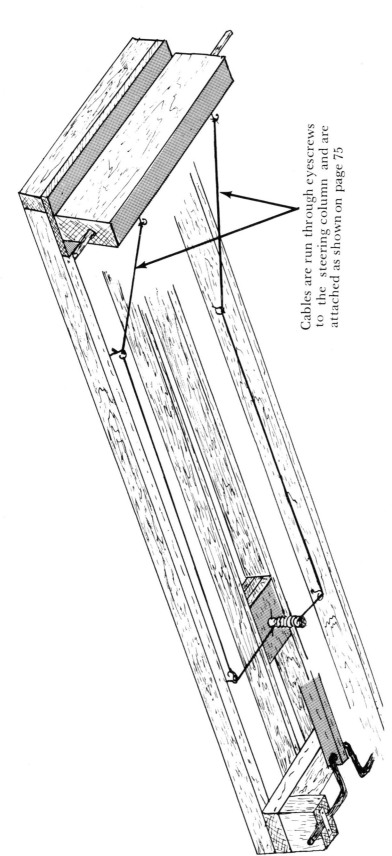

Cables are run through eyescrews to the steering column and are attached as shown on page 75

Handcar rear axle tree and connecting bar for axle type C

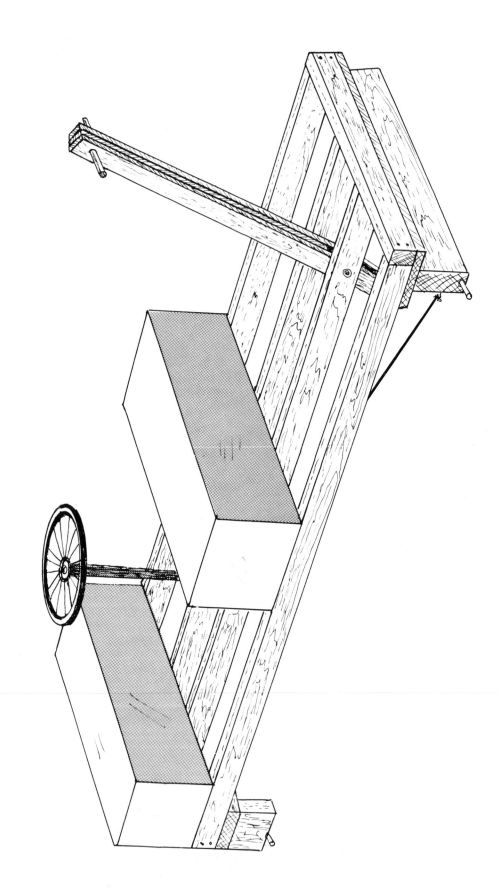

STEERING COLUMN AND WHEEL IN POSITION
BOX SEATS INSTALLED

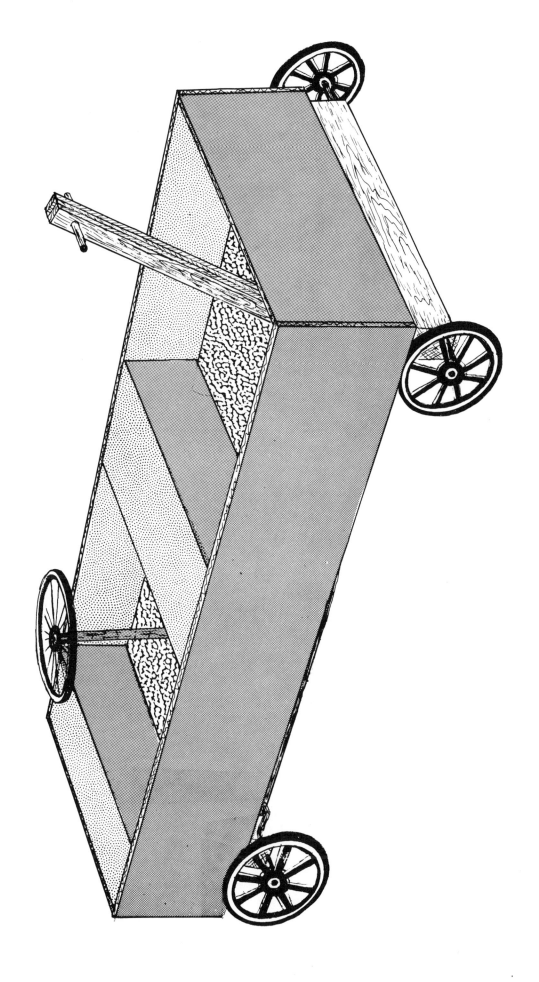

Two-Man sidewalk handcar